The High Road

The High Road

Compiled and edited by

Duane Mehl, Ph.D.

Parkside Publishing Corporation

205 West Touhy Avenue
Park Ridge, IL 60068

Mehl, Duane
    The High Road
ISBN 0-942421-05-1
Printed in the United States of America
10   9   8   7

Table of Contents

Introduction

This book is dedicated to all persons everywhere who suffer or are recovering from addiction to alcohol or other mood-altering drugs. It is also dedicated to all persons who may love and depend upon people addicted to alcohol or other drugs.

The book is the creation of many people, men and women, young and old, rich and poor, professionals with high status and people without status or even employment. What the contributors have in common is experience with addiction in their own lives, in the lives of people they love, or in the lives of people they have served while working as staff members at alcoholism and drug abuse treatment centers. The authors share a dread of addiction, but also a belief that the disease can be arrested, and that life and well being can be restored both to those who abuse mood-altering chemicals and to those who love and depend upon the abusers.

Because the experience of addiction is so complex, it can and should be described in many different ways. Though all alcoholics and addicts experience loss of control over mood-altering substances, each addict experiences that loss uniquely. Age, gender, family ties, work, emotional stability, sexuality, self-image, and general life situation all shape the particular way in which the disease of addiction affects peoples' behavior and lives.

With that in mind, the writers of *The High Road* have tried to address the needs of all alcoholics and those addicted to other drugs. The writers also address certain issues not often treated in print and other media: sexuality and addiction, cross-addiction to more than one drug, addiction and its impact on divorced people, or on persons experiencing crises such as illness, severe loss and failure, or the threat of death. The writers have tried in each chapter to remember that "alcoholism is a family disease," affecting not only the person addicted, but those close to him or her, and especially those who love and are dependent upon him or her.

This book has been written to read and use. Brief introductions are offered at the beginning of each chapter to help the reader quickly grasp the reason the chapter has been included. Most of the contributors have written in the first person, honestly and directly. To assist readers, staff members of treatment centers, or participants in a group to "work" with the material in the book, questions, tests and other methods for personal evaluation and sharing with others have been provided with every chapter. The first chapter, "Is It Time to Worry About Your Drinking?" begins with a brief list of carefully chosen questions to help you determine whether you or your loved ones may have a problem with drinking or drugs.

We hope the contents of *The High Road* will help addicted people and those who love them *up* from the down road of alcohol and other drug dependence. We would be less than honest if we did not say that addiction is a terribly complicated and difficult illness, or if we pretended that it is simple or easy to begin and maintain recovery from the illness. We would be even more dishonest, however, if we pretended there is no hope for recovery.

Millions of recovering people and family members attest to that hope daily by their continuing sobriety, productivity, and happiness. Thousands of people, working in alcohol and drug abuse treatment centers today, believe and know from experience that recovery is possible for their patients and guests. Thousands of Alcoholics Anonymous and Narcotics Anonymous members, gathering everywhere in the world to sustain their recovery, say at the end of their meetings: "Keep coming back. It works, if you work it!" In that spirit, we have written our book.

1

Is It Time To Worry About Your Drinking?

INTRODUCTION

In a society where alcohol and other mood-altering drugs are regularly consumed in social settings, many people have difficulty determining and admitting to themselves and others that they are having problems with their drinking or drug use. Family members and friends of heavy drinking or drug-using people have similar difficulties in making a diagnosis of the problems of others.

This chapter is designed to prevent you from passing "judgment" either too early or too late upon your own or someone else's drinking and drug use. With the disease of addiction, diagnosis and identification of a problem are critically important for initiating recovery. Please read the following questions and answer them honestly. If your answers to the questions indicate that you or others have a problem with alcohol or other drugs, it is time for you to read the rest of the chapter.

THE QUESTIONS

If you answer three or more of these questions "yes" you do have a problem with drinking or drugs and need to have an evaluation at a treatment center or to talk to someone associated with Alcoholics Anonymous.

1. I usually have difficulty feeling comfortable at social gatherings unless I am slightly high.

2. Sometimes I use alcohol or drugs because I am anxious or to fall asleep.

3. Sometimes when I drink or use drugs my personality changes. I become hostile, aggressive, withdrawn or think I am the life of the party.

4. My spouse, family members or friends have told me that I am drinking or using drugs too much.

5. I regularly use cocaine, alcohol or other drugs to heighten my sexual enjoyment.

6. When I drink or use drugs I no longer seem able to stop when I want to.

7. I have quit drinking or using drugs for awhile to prove that I could, or to keep a promise.

8. My drinking or using drugs is causing family problems.

9. Sometimes I hide my supply or sneak drinks or drugs.

10. I feel guilt or shame about my drinking or drug use and have wondered at times if I have a problem.

11. Sometimes I wake up after heavy drinking or drugging and can't remember everything that happened.

PERSONALLY SPEAKING

Since I am a recovering alcoholic, I shall speak in part of my own experiences with alcoholism. Since I have also worked for some years as a counselor in private practice, I can also, without breaking confidences, draw upon the general experiences of many other alcoholics when I ask the question: Is it time to worry about your drinking?

Unfortunately, I know of no more sensitive subject in human society than this one. We may talk more easily today about sex, politics, or religion, than about symptoms of alcoholic drinking or abuse of mood-altering drugs. And there is a reason. Since so many people consume alcoholic beverages and other drugs, very few people like to be reminded that they have lost control over the consumption of their mood-altering chemicals.

Nonetheless, millions of people this very day wonder or worry secretly over the question: Am I an alcoholic? An addict? Is my husband, wife, parent, child, an alcoholic? How can I find out quietly, on my own? I hope this chapter will help you discover whether you and/or your loved one are presently drinking or drugging in an addictive pattern. I'm positive it won't hurt to keep on reading.

PATTERN AND PURPOSE

To my way of thinking, problem drinking exists whenever anyone becomes concerned or worried about his own or someone else's drinking.

Now we shall not hear much of such symptoms from the non-alcoholic experts who chart the descent into alcoholism. Perhaps, we hear so little about initial symptoms because drinkers carefully hide those symptoms from others. They do not show up on the diagnostic charts, because the problem drinker virtually forgets how it all started.

In my middle twenties, for instance, I had begun to drink almost every night before going to bed. Though I went out with friends from graduate school who seemed to drink as much as I did, somewhere along the line I thought to myself: I'm drinking every night in order to go to sleep and stay asleep. The thought made me vaguely uncomfortable. I didn't say to myself, I'm becoming an alcoholic. Rather, I thought, I've got to stop this one of these days.

I had begun to drink in a regular pattern, for a definite purpose: sleep. And since I became conscious of the pattern and purpose, I also became slightly preoccupied—that is, I felt slightly uneasy about my drinking.

I was then far from being an alcoholic. Had I cut down on my drinking then, or stopped, I would have had no further problems. But the earliest sign I detected was a pattern, and a non-social purpose for my drinking.

> *. . . all began . . . to drink in a regular pattern for a specific purpose, and became preoccupied about it.*

I have since talked to dozens of alcoholics who have "confessed" to exactly the same kind of experiences. Not all drank to go to sleep—though a large number of alcoholics get into trouble that way. Some drank to "wind down" from a day on the job. Some drank in the afternoon to overcome feelings of boredom and loneliness. Some drank on weekends to seek release from tension, and for "pleasure." But all began at some time to drink in a regular pattern for a specific purpose, and became preoccupied about it.

TOLERANCE

As I continued to drink, I also discovered that I needed a little more alcohol each successive month to put me soundly to sleep. Pill users may experience the same need: more pills, or other drugs, to produce the same feelings.

The experts call this feeling tolerance. People headed for addiction build up a tolerance for their drug of choice. As a result, they feel as if they need more than they consumed when they first began to use the drug.

The ability to consume large amounts of alcohol or other drugs without showing effect, is an early sign of possible alcoholism or addiction. The heavy, "two-fisted" drinker, who holds his or her liquor well, is quite possibly a man or woman on the way to alcoholism.

Much of the legendary lore celebrating the art and craft of drinking is, quite frankly, a bunch of baloney. Problem drinkers protect themselves by pretending their ability to consume large amounts of alcohol is a virtue. As a matter of fact, it's a real danger signal. We are much better off if we don't have a high tolerance for alcohol.

SNEAKING AND GULPING

When drinkers or drug users begin to use more than before, most of them also begin to sneak and gulp drinks or other drugs. Even when the addictive person uses mood-altering chemicals in social settings, at parties or at home among family members, he or she will begin to use on the sly.

Why? Because we don't feel quite right about those amounts we consume. Unless all of our friends consume very heavily, we really don't want to stand out like a sore thumb.

When I was married and working, I still drank socially, but too heavily for me to feel comfortable about it. As a result I drank a couple of bottles of beer openly with my wife, but drank another couple privately out in the garage, or in my home office where I thought my wife wouldn't notice me. At parties, I began sneaking drinks out of the bottle when nobody else was looking. Before the party began, I would have a little nip, and then afterwards, have another nip before going to bed. Do you know what I mean?

If you drink at a bar among heavy-drinking friends, you may not have to hide anything from them. But if you're married, and come home afterwards to a spouse, you tell him or her you had a "couple" of beers or maybe martinis (often dependent upon your financial situation), when in fact you drank a whole case of beer, or downed nine or ten vodkas straight, with or without the rocks.

You may begin also to worry about the money you spend on alcohol, or on doctors and prescription drugs, or on the drugs you buy from dealers in your school, your workplace, your favorite bar, or off the streets.

BLACKOUTS

Somewhere along the line, I began to forget the next morning exactly what happened at the party. Not only could I not remember what others said after 10:00 P.M., but I couldn't remember what I said. In fact, I couldn't remember exactly whether I was at the party at all after 10:00 P.M.

That is the strangest experience. It makes you feel very sheepish and guilty and afraid. In fact, you feel so guilty and fearful that you say nothing to anyone about the memory loss. Instead, you try to find out what happened. You casually but carefully ask your wife or husband or some other close person, "What exactly happened at the party while I was outside taking a long walk for a breath of fresh air?"

If someone tells you that you didn't take a walk, but tried to stand on your head, and fell into your best friend's china cabinet, you don't say, I did? You say, Gosh, wasn't that awful? I have to pay for all that broken china. And when your wife or husband then says, but honey, you didn't break anything, don't you remember? You say quickly, of course I remember. I was just speaking "metaphorically." I mean I have to apologize to my friends, or something like that.

Notice, we alcoholics learn to lie and alibi very early in the drinking game. If we keep on drinking it gets much worse.

Some of us who drink in the afternoons or at other odd hours, may talk on the telephone and forget both the telephone call and the conversation afterwards. And that creates a lot of problems. Especially if we negotiate a business deal on the phone, or proposition our neighbor's wife or husband.

Experts and Alcoholics Anonymous members call these experiences "blackouts," which may be a poor choice of words. When problem drinkers read about blackouts, they usually think that means, "passing out." And since they're not passing out, they think they have no real problems.

A blackout, however, means a simple loss of memory experienced by a drinker or drug user, who, while conscious, consumes enough alcohol or other drugs to interfere with memory.

> *Loss of control . . . the drinker or drug*
> *user consumes more and more with*
> *less effect . . . and . . . can't pre-*
> *dict . . . how much he will consume.*

THE TURNING POINT—LOSS OF CONTROL

If a heavy drinker decides after experiencing these symptoms that it's time to cut back drastically on the drinking, he or she can sometimes control consumption and avoid the descent into chronic alcoholism.

If you drink in this pattern, therefore, you should try to do everything possible to interrupt the pattern and cut down on consumption. If not, you may move on to the next stage: loss of control over consumption of alcohol and/or other drugs.

Loss of control is best described by what fails to happen. As the drinker or drug user consumes more and more with less effect, he discovers that after the first drink or pill, or line of cocaine, he can't predict any longer how much he will consume. He can't predict just how long he will keep drinking or drugging. And worst of all, he can't predict how he will act under the influence of his favorite drug.

This is an awful experience—but also a key to identifying alcoholism or addiction in yourself or in someone close to you.

By definition, an alcoholic does not know exactly what's going to happen after he or she begins to consume alcohol or mood-altering chemicals. There are other definitions of alcoholism, but this one is my favorite.

Once we alcoholics lose control, we can only very rarely cut back or by ourselves abstain from alcohol or other drugs. When drinking or drugging we lose our power of will over ourselves. Unless we find help, we shall get progressively worse in our drinking and drugging and shall eventually go crazy, die, or both.

By the above definition, I by no means imply that all persons experiencing loss of control drink until they pass out. When I drank alcoholicly, I usually consumed white wine, and stayed on my feet, taught classes on a graduate level, attended faculty and administrative meetings, and even advanced somewhat up the ladder of vocational success.

A woman friend of mine—also a wine drinker—sought help in a treatment center without ever experiencing a single awkward moment in a public or social situation. At parties and similar gatherings she always drank very carefully. During the afternoons in her own home, however, she regularly drank sherry, and often found herself unable to function soberly when her family members came home from school and work.

By her own calculation, she had become alcoholic, and with the help of others, now abstains from alcohol completely.

She and I were what some experts call functioning alcoholics, balmy just about everyday, but able to function reasonably well when trying to fulfill not-too-demanding responsibilities.

Thousands of men and women all over the world do the same with wine, liquor, beer, pills, and pot in a variety of settings. We learn to consume just enough to keep ourselves high without knocking ourselves out.

However, since we are regularly under the influence of drugs that affect our central nervous system, we function as impaired people. We cut down on our abilities to act like responsible adults. And we damage our bodies, our minds, and our emotions.

Many alcoholics drink on a periodic basis—often on weekends, on vacations or holidays, or at parties—and abstain the rest of the time. However, when they drink on weekends or at parties, they usually lose control of their consumption.

They may also disappear from the house for days and spend large sums of money. Maybe they will drink two days straight, sleep for 24 hours, and then abstain for a while again. No matter how infrequently they drink, however, they lose control.

Neither the amount nor the timing of your drug consumption necessarily determines whether you are addicted. A close friend of mine drank only a six-pack of beer on Friday nights after work. Always on those evenings, however, he became both drunk and abusive in his behavior toward his wife.

Because he drank relatively little and only on weekends, he refused for many years to admit that he had a "problem." Only after his wife finally divorced him on grounds of chronic "drunkenness" and physical cruelty did he finally get the message. He was an alcoholic with a low tolerance for alcohol. After spending a month in treatment, he has with the help of AA remained sober for several years.

He paid a price for his drinking, however, that you may not have to pay if you are willing to admit to yourself as early as possible the problems you create with alcohol or similar drugs.

ALIBIING

When an alcoholic drinks out of control, he experiences constant guilt over his behavior and tries therefore all the harder to alibi for it—that is, he hides the evidence of sick behavior as best he can. He lies and alibis like crazy. In fact, as he continues to drink out of control, he gets so much in the habit of lying and alibiing that neither he nor his family members can tell the difference any longer between truth and falsehood.

Unfortunately, the majority of alcoholics in time become chronic liars about everything. Because they feel their world falling apart, they become grandiose about themselves, always exaggerating their abilities and accomplishments, shading the truth about every aspect of their existence to protect themselves against the terrible truth; they are now eliminating their capacity for moral judgments, destroying everything near and dear to them, and inexorably drinking themselves to death.

PROTECTING SUPPLY

Most alcoholics, for instance, pretend to drink or drug far less than they really do. As a result, they constantly minimize amounts they consume outside the house, and hide their supply of booze inside the house.

Alcoholics learn to hide bottles or drugs in any and every place they can think of. I hid wine bottles in clothes drawers, clothes hampers, suitcases, under the mattress of my bed, over heating ducts in the basement, on strings from rafters in the attic, in trees, under bushes and underground outside, in garbage cans, car trunks, under the car hood, in my children's toy box, and in the piano.

One of the chapters in *The High Road* describes a woman who buried bottles at ground level in her backyard where she could sun bathe on her side, and sip alcohol out of the ground with a straw. I have known of women and men who hid alcohol in cleaner bottles—any bottle with color enough to conceal the booze.

This is known by experts as "protecting supply." It is mean and ornery stuff—big-time lying for the alcoholic and terribly painful both for him or her, and for the family members. The behavior is also a red flag symptom of alcoholism. How many normal drinkers you know hide bottles from strings attached to the rafters in their attic?

My wife and children, of course, knew full well I was hiding bottles and drinking on the sly. Not only did they see it in my eyes, detect it in my movements, and smell it on my breath—they found my carefully hidden bottles all over the house all the time.

My son and daughter in particular—about nine and ten years of age at the time—became experts at finding my bottles. And together both my family and I became sicker and sicker as a result of my behavior.

ABSTINENCE

Almost all alcoholics also decide from time to time to prove to themselves and others that they can abstain for a while. Most alcoholics and other types of drug addicts can manage without drugs for short periods of time. After proving they can manage, however, the majority then celebrate their abstinence by drinking out of control again.

If you feel the desire to prove yourself non-alcoholic by abstaining for a little while, you have probably proved yourself alcoholic just by the thought and decision alone. How many normal drinkers you know decide they have to prove themselves normal by abstaining from alcohol? I've never met one. Whereas every alcoholic I have known has tried to abstain, done so successfully for a while—sometimes for months—then returned, only to discover that with the first drink or drug he or she has no more control than before.

If a heavy drinker can consume one, two, or three ounces daily for a period of several months without increasing consumption, he may have proved he has control. However, if you try that test, don't fool yourself and others by using tranquilizing drugs, sleeping pills, pot, or any other drug on the side. Those other drugs neatly displace the need for alcohol, while fulfilling the same requirement.

LOSS OF MORAL JUDGMENT

As the drinker or drug user continues to consume out of control, alibiing constantly for his behavior, he begins to lose the capacity to make judgments about right and wrong behavior. Because the drinker now needs alcohol or other drugs in order to function, he loses his ability to function responsibly toward himself and other people.

For example, most alcoholics drink and drive. Years ago when I gave lectures to patients in treatment centers about loss of moral judgment I asked two questions: How many of you drove when you were drunk? Almost every person would raise a hand. Then I asked: How many of you think it is wrong to drive while drinking? Almost every person would also raise a hand.

Knowing it is morally wrong, alcoholic people continue to drive when drinking. Knowing full well we endanger the lives of people, we drive anyhow. We could multiply this example a hundred times over.

. . . the drinker or drug user creates problems for himself or herself at work and relationships with family members.

Though we know it is morally irresponsible to go to work half drunk or with a hangover, we do it repeatedly. Though we know when drinking we constantly fail in the most elementary responsibilities of work, play, and basic responsibilities toward our spouses and other family members, we keep on drinking.

When drinking, we become moody and withdrawn, or grandiose and aggressive. We may threaten our family with violence, or hide from our family in remorse. And though we fail to measure up to our own standards of behavior, we keep on drinking anyhow.

Failure to measure up to personal standards of behavior may, in fact, be one of the hardest things an alcoholic or addict has to bear. It is no wonder that he or she finally becomes almost constantly anxious, depressed, and filled with vague fears about everything conceivable. It is no wonder that the addicted person becomes "paranoid," fearful that everyone is judging him, or that someone or something is out to get him.

Guilt helps to produce these feelings. Unfortunately, the alcoholic knows full well that alcohol or other drugs temporarily relieves those awful feelings. After a while, in fact, the alcoholic or drug addict actually drinks and drugs to relieve symptoms produced by drinking and drugging. If that sounds like crazy behavior, I can assure you it is. The alcoholic, however, feels that he has no choice. If he stops, he thinks that those bad feelings will overwhelm him and truly drive him crazy.

PROBLEMS WITH JOB AND FAMILY

Early in the downward descent into addiction, the drinker or drug user creates problems for himself or herself at work, in relationships with family members, or in other crucially important areas of life.

If you cause such problems for yourself through your consumption, you would do well to visit a treatment center for consultation, or an AA meeting, to learn more about why you continue to create such difficulties.

If you experience such problems, please don't waste your time and others trying to determine whether you are or are not alcoholic. You do best to assume you need help, rather than continue to deteriorate.

THINGS TO COME

If you keep on drinking and drugging without adequate control over yourself, you will probably in time start drinking when you get up from sleep. Why? To eliminate symptoms of hangover—of drug and alcohol withdrawal—especially the "shakes."

You will spend outrageous sums of money, not only on alcohol and other drugs, but upon doctors and lawyers you will need to help you out of difficulties you create while intoxicated.

You will lose the respect and company of your friends and family members. Even your buddies down at the bar or club may no longer want to associate with you. In response, you may choose to drink always alone, or go to strange bars and taverns in bad sections of town seeking out drunken people who will "accept" you as you are—which means, people who drink like you drink.

Because your spouse or other partner may refuse to have sexual relations with you on a regular basis, you may be driven to seek out other lonely men or women, prostitutes, or "studs" hanging around bars, trying to prove to yourself that you're still sexually acceptable to someone.

You may have accidents with your car and hurt yourself and others. You will begin to get citations for drunk driving, and may spend time in jail. You will begin to hurt yourself, and your family members, even your pets around the home. In time, your family members—if they stick with you—will have to place you in hospitals for "checkups," for "drying out," or for treatment of physical ailments—hypertension, liver disease, or many other illnesses—hoping that you will finally abstain and get better.

Unless you seek help, you will begin to lose not only one job, but others as well. Your spouse may leave you and seek a divorce. Your children may decide they never want to speak to you again, or ever look at your bleary and bloated face.

Addiction is not child's play. It is a deadly illness, characterized by loss of control over alcohol or similar drugs, leading to failure in responsible living. Unless interrupted, it eventually leads to physical, emotional, and spiritual deterioration and finally collapse.

> *If we keep on drinking, we decide, in effect, to commit suicide with continuing use of alcohol or other drugs.*

COLLAPSE

When an alcoholic or addict collapses or gives up, he or she drinks and drugs with reckless abandon, no longer even trying to stop. To my way of thinking, this is the fate worse than death facing any addicted person.

If we keep on drinking, we decide, in effect, to commit suicide with continuing use of alcohol or other drugs. It is a feeling beyond description. I know because I've had the feeling. I fear it more than insanity or death by alcohol consumption, which, however, will come inevitably, if I drink again.

If you have reached that point in your drinking and have literally thought you would rather die than keep on consuming, you may, however, still change your mind. With the help of others, you may find yourself ready to admit you're powerless over alcohol or other drugs.

Take my word for it, you still have a good chance for recovery. I have known hundreds of alcoholics in AA who have reached this bottom rung and, with the help of a treatment center staff, abstinence, lifetime attendance at AA, and work with the AA program of recovery, have been restored to normal living. Many AA members I know have become *better* spiritually and emotionally than they were before they lost control over their drinking.

THE FINAL HOPE

If you presently despair of recovery from your drinking and drugging problems, I want to offer you one great word of hope: many people who go down the drain with alcohol and other drugs, come up again to the surface and beyond. In the words of the late Karl Menninger, the psychiatrist, they become "weller than well," more peaceful, serene, and loving then they could ever have been before they began their descent into addiction.

Though you may not believe it now, you can, with the help of others, come to know that reality later. Why not try to discover resources for your recovery right now? You have nothing to lose but your chains. Talk it over with people near and dear to you. Reach for the phone and call your local AA number, or a treatment center. The life you save will be your own.

Questions for: *Is It Time To Worry About Your Drinking?*

1. Almost all alcoholics and other addicts begin using the drugs of their choice in a regular pattern for non-social purposes. What was your pattern of use?

2. Did you develop a "tolerance" for alcohol or other drugs of your choice? If so, describe your experiences.

3. When did you begin to sneak and gulp drinks, or other drugs? How did you go about it?

4. Did you experience blackouts under the influence of alcohol or other drugs? Describe your experiences.

5. Did you ever violate your own moral standards under the in-

fluence of alcohol or other drugs? Give examples of your experiences.

6. Have you ever despaired of getting better, and secretly decided just to keep on drinking or drugging forever? Describe your feelings. Do you think you can get better now? How?

2

Honesty, the Policy of Power

INTRODUCTION

The Big Book of Alcoholics Anonymous contains the following words about recovering from alcoholism: "Rarely have we seen a person fail who has thoroughly followed our path. Those who do not recover are people who cannot or will not completely give themselves to this simple program, usually men and women who are constitutionally incapable of being honest with themselves . . . They are naturally incapable of grasping and developing a manner of living which demands rigorous honesty. Their chances are less than average."[*]

When we first heard those words in an AA meeting, we felt a twinge of terror in our hearts, "Maybe I'm one of those people constitutionally incapable of being honest with themselves." We promptly became depressed over the thought.

Both the thought and the feeling of depression, however, proved we were capable of honesty after all. If a recovering alcoholic worries about being honest, he or she is already, without knowing it, recognizing personal shortcomings and getting honest with himself or herself. And with honesty comes the possibility for continuing recovery from addiction. So we believe.

What has worked for us may work for you also. We write in this chapter, about our experiences as addicted men and women with the absolutely vital ingredient of honesty for recovery from addiction; and we recommend our hard-earned lessons to you. Though we don't know whether all of you—especially those in the early stages of recovery—

[*]From Chapter 5 of *Alcoholics Anonymous*. Reprinted with permission.

will agree with our convictions about the spiritual basis for honesty during sobriety, we do ask you to hear us out, and then examine the questions at the conclusion of this chapter.

THE ROOTS OF DISHONESTY

Among recovering alcoholics, honesty shows itself most obviously in the willingness to admit powerlessness over alcohol. The founders of Alcoholics Anonymous placed so much weight upon honesty as the foundation of recovery because, first, they had discovered no alcoholic ever recovers unless he or she honestly admits he or she is an alcoholic. Second, they discovered no alcoholic continues to recover unless he or she develops a genuine capacity for honesty throughout life.

As we began to experience sobriety, that way of life was tough for us even to imagine and for a very simple reason. When we drank we lied not only about the amounts, the pattern, the expense, and the results of our drinking and drug use, but with a gathering sense of necessity, we shaded the truth about everything we thought and did. Once we began to lie, we learned that one lie often requires another covering lie, which leads to another.

Since alcohol or other drugs had become the most important thing in life for us, we had to pretend day after day that all the other things connected with jobs and relationships were not only similarly important, but were proceeding normally.

On the simplest level, we continued to tell our wives or husbands we loved them as much as ever when in fact we gradually lost the capacity to care for anyone except ourselves and our next drink, pill, or snort of cocaine. Unfortunately, alcohol or similar drugs tend to mask or even eliminate an addict's feelings of love for other people. To "prove" our love for our spouse, for instance, we may have talked as if we were succeeding at our work to help support our families— when in fact we often failed in our work, or jeopardized our jobs, and if necessary would probably have given them up for the sake of the bottle.

> *Among recovering alcoholics honesty shows itself most obviously in the willingness to admit powerlessness over alcohol.*

Had we never discovered the need to admit our powerlessness over the bottle, we might have become some of those people which the Big Book describes as incapable of being honest. Had we not admitted our defeat by alcohol, we would never have admitted to any other moral, emotional, or physical defeats in our lives either. We would have remained not only thoroughly powerless but also thoroughly dishonest persons.

THE BEGINNING OF HONESTY

Since we alcoholics tend to lie about almost everything when we're drinking, and feel constantly guilty about it, we must in recovery, gradually become as truthful as we can.

Recovery from alcoholism began with our honest self-admission of powerlessness over alcohol and life. Recovery from alcoholism continued with our honest acceptance, one day at a time, of help from persons and powers outside of ourselves for recovery from addiction.

Honesty is the policy of power for us recovering alcoholics. We admitted we were powerless over alcohol, and then found ourselves able to turn to powers greater than ourselves for help. In that sentence, we believe, lies the secret to sobriety, and of peace and happiness, among our fellow human beings.

THE PRACTICE OF HONESTY

If you truly wish to learn the secrets of sobriety and grow in a healthy and loving way among other people, you must also make every effort to be honest in both your thoughts and actions day by day.

Notice first that we say, "thoughts." If we cannot be honest with our innermost self, we can never come close to being honest in our relationships with others.

We try to practice honesty every day simply by turning each day over into the hands of our Higher Power—which some of us think of as God, while others think of as their AA group—and saying, "I can't successfully manage it all by myself. Help!" We end each day by reflecting briefly upon our thoughts and actions, by sharing our mistakes with God or our Higher Power, as we best understand Him or it, and asking for the power to sleep and to do better the next day.

And always we pray at the beginning and the end of the day to remain sober. For without sobriety, we can be honest about nothing.

We try to be honest one day at a time. Like sobriety, rigorous honesty is best practiced on a daily basis. If we vow to be honest for a lifetime, we simply set ourselves up for a fall and subsequent guilt. If we pray to be honest for one day, we allow powers and people greater than ourselves to help us toward reasonable success that day.

We find that we can practice honesty to the degree that we can accept our limitations. When we cannot accept our limitations, we automatically lie in order to inflate ourselves and our accomplishments. For recovering alcoholics and addicts, nothing could be more insidious than such habits of self-inflation. When we lie about ourselves, we feel uneasy. And when we feel uneasy, we begin to set ourselves up for another mood-altering drink or drug.

Many of us use the Serenity Prayer on a daily basis to help us maintain a healthy sobriety. *"God grant me the serenity to accept the things I cannot change, courage to change the things I can, and the wisdom to know the difference."*

We believe that prayer beautifully sums up our needs for God's help to remain honest, and thereby to accept our limitations and weaknesses, as well as our strengths, day by day.

Like sobriety, rigorous honesty is best practiced on a daily basis.

HONESTY IN SMALL AND LARGE THINGS

We pray for the power to be honest in the smaller things in order to gain the ability to be honest in the larger things. Many of us, in fact, discover that we can paradoxically be honest more easily in large than in small matters.

In recovery, for instance, some of us found that we could more easily tell others that we had once stolen bottles of wine from a grocery store—a felony—than we could say, "I just lied to my best friend about my salary. I told him I make $5,000 more than I really do."

Do you sense what we mean? That little "white lie" may become the beginning of many more lies, which in time will trap us and lead us back where we started—to drinking for relief.

When we were drinking and drugging, we lied about both the small and the large realities of our lives. Many of us reached the point where we literally could not resist the urge to exaggerate or fabricate everything we said—particularly about our feelings and our accomplishments in life.

Because we were failing so miserably, we often felt an obsessive need to pretend to others that we were succeeding in our work beyond our wildest dreams. Often, we pretended to feel much more "sexy" than we were remotely capable of feeling, in order to compensate for our loss of feeling under the influence. Now, in recovery, we believe we must for the sake of spiritual health, try as much as possible to be rigorously honest about everything we feel and do.

When we stop telling people, for instance, that we make more money than we actually do—when we accept simple realities about ourselves and our lives—we find ourselves more easily telling the truth about everything.

When we tell the literal truth about ourselves, we know also that we have accepted ourselves and others for what they are. As we came, through association with other people in AA, to believe a Power greater than ourselves also accepts us as we are, we found it just that much easier to accept ourselves and the whole world as it is.

After we have been sober for a while . . . we must try with all our might to stop condemning others . . .

Honesty is the foundation of spirituality. Honesty allows us to accept the person in our own mirror, exist in fellowship with the God of our understanding, and live freely and openly with other people. And as we develop good relationships with others, we discover that we have fewer and fewer reasons for lying about ourselves, and for turning to alcohol or other drugs for relief.

HOW HONEST ARE YOU?

Try the following questions. If you find yourself answering "yes" to more than a few, you may have a tendency to be dishonest about yourself. As you abuse alcohol or other drugs, you will undoubtedly increase your tendency to lie about your life.

1. I regularly try to convince people that I have more power, influence, and appeal than I actually have.

2. In my work, school, or business, I pretend to successes and status which I do not have.

3. I make up or elaborate stories about people in order to get other people's attention.

4. When I lie outright and am caught, I usually "minimize" the lie. For example: Laughingly I say, "By a couple of beers, I really meant a couple of cases. Ha, ha," and so forth.

5. At the bar, I sometimes buy a round to pretend to other people that things are better in my life than they really are.

6. I have parties which I cannot really afford in order to impress other people.

7. Because I am constantly envious of certain other people, I run them down and pretend that I am better than they are.

8. I constantly pretend to have feelings which I do not have, such as appreciation or respect for others, sympathy, or even love.

9. I find myself regularly lying to family members and even my friends about the amounts, the cost, and the results of my drinking and drugging.

You can think of many other examples of dishonesty from your own life, which will help you complete what AA calls your "moral inventory"—your personal assessment of tendencies toward dishonesty. Remember: recovery from alcoholism and other forms of addiction depends, above everything else, upon your total honesty about yourself.

LIVE AND LET LIVE

Honesty about our personal weaknesses and wrongs always turns our critical judgment inward, and makes it difficult for us to judge and reject other people for their weaknesses and wrongs. As a recovering alcoholic progresses in his or her program, he or she will frequently say about persons less fortunate, "There but by the grace of God go I." Given slightly different curcumstances, I could very well be in his or her shoes.

If the words sound corny to you, they may sound that way because you have not yet become thoroughly honest about your life. When we first began to attend meetings, some sayings in AA sounded corny to us also. When we began to recognize and share our weaknesses with others, however, we began also to sense that we were recovering not by our own power, or by "coincidence," but with the help of others— that is, by God's grace.

As one of our alcoholic friends likes to say, "Coincidence is God's way of remaining anonymous."

Since we know deep down inside that we are not naturally better than others, we realize instinctively that we could very well be the worst of others. Since we know that we are capable of doing many of the wrong things that other people do—while drinking we may already have done so!—we cannot help but feel that a power greater than ourselves has enabled us to find the road to recovery and well-being.

But how can a recovering alcoholic reduce his or her habit of judging others, and concentrate instead upon self-improvement?

HOW BAD HABITS DEVELOP

When drinking, most of us alcoholics still know and even feel the differences between right and wrong thoughts and actions. We tend to display our knowledge of morality, however, by regularly judging and condemning others.

For instance: to protect ourselves against criticism for drunken behavior, we married alcoholics usually managed to find fault first and foremost with our sober wives or husbands. To protect ourselves against criticism, we became experts at projecting our faults upon all the people close to us—not only family members, but also our employers, employees, clients, or, if in business our ourselves, upon our customers.

Some of us in small businesses became absolutely "convinced" that we drank because of nasty customers! We also drank because the weather was good or bad, because the economy was up or down, because we cooked a good or a lousy meal, because our kids were sick or healthy, because our football team won or lost. Do you remember how that works? It's all a lie, of course. In reality, we had lost control over our consumption of alcohol. We drank because we wanted and needed to drink. For a chronic alcoholic, the reason for drinking finally becomes almost that simple.

Unfortunately any alcoholic, married and working for a living, has plenty of people and things to blame for his or her drinking. How many marriages are really made in heaven? And who on earth really likes his or her work all of the time? Who really gets along with the boss all of the time?

Since our continuing sobriety depends upon our capacity for honesty, however, we alcoholics can no longer afford to project our faults on other people, or upon events or things happening in our lives. After we have been sober for a while, we believe we must try with all our might to stop judging and condemning others—especially our family members or other important people in our lives.

As Christ once said, "Judge not, and you will not be judged" by others. When we stop judging other people, they find it that much easier to stop judging us also. And freedom from judgments and criticism makes it so much easier for us alcoholics to stay happily sober day by day.

Obviously, none of us ever succeeds fully in avoiding judgments of others. If we want to live and let live, however, we'll try to concentrate on our own faults, and leave the faults of others to God as we understand Him. We thereby prove to ourselves that we have to some degree given up our moralistic criticism of others, and become critical of our own real defects of character.

MORAL, NOT MORALISM

Moralistic criticism is something we had always directed at other people. When we began in sobriety to learn real morality, we began to direct our critical judgment first toward ourselves. We tried to take our own "moral inventory." When we understood and tried to correct our own faults first, we began also to understand the faults of other people with whom we shared similar faults.

. . . in a curiously refreshing way,
rigorous honesty made us hard on
ourselves and accepting of others.

Does that make sense to you? We gained true insight into the wrongs of others when we realized that we had committed similar wrongs, though perhaps in somewhat different ways and degrees.

As moral philosophers, past and present, tell us: murder begins with anger and hate, sexual promiscuity begins with simple desire to take advantage of another for sexual self-gratification, theft begins with the desire to have something another owns, and character assassination often begins with nothing more than simple gossip.

Given the circumstance and provocation, we were, while drinking, probably capable of doing, or at least thinking about doing, anything that anybody else might do. Even in sobriety, the thoughts continued to come. Thus, in a curiously refreshing way, rigorous honesty made us hard on ourselves and accepting of others. In fact, we know some recovering people, very advanced in spiritual growth, who cannot ultimately reject any human being for his or her wrongs, because they see the potential for similar wrongs in themselves. They try to remember St. Augustine's advice to hate the "sin" but love the "sinner."

We do not mean to suggest that recovering alcoholics sanction evil behavior. In recovery, we may become, in fact, more conscious of human capacity for evil than ever before. However, since we know first hand about human weakness, we naturally tend to separate human beings from the evil they bring about. We learn to forgive ourselves more easily, even though we remain highly conscious of our capacity to wrong others. As we continue to forgive and accept ourselves for our past faults, we finally develop by God's grace the ability to forgive and accept others.

Honesty comes with humility and humility comes with honesty.

Tough Love

Many of us recovering alcoholics believe God, as we understand Him, acts toward people in the same way. If a good God judges our real wrongs, He also chooses to forgive. For that reason some alcoholics we know call God "Tough Love," or "T.L." To follow God's lead, as we understand Him, we recovering alcoholics hold ourselves and even others accountable for real wrong we or they did during and after our drinking, especially when we sponsor another person in the AA fellowship. But we also continue to accept each other, and look forward daily to the possibility, with God's help, of improvement in our behavior and growth in our spiritual life.

We practice tough love upon each other. We don't expect perfection, but we do expect spiritual growth in ourselves and others. As the Big Book says of the AA way of life: "No one among us has been able to maintain anything like perfect adherence to these principles. We are not saints. The point is, that we are willing to grow along spiritual lines. The principles we have set down are guides to progress rather than spiritual perfection."

With that attitude we try to pursue another of the great virtues necessary for recovery: humility. In fact, honesty comes with humility and humility comes with honesty. With a combination of both, we can ask each day that God remove our defects of character, and allow us to admit to our future wrongs with ease and grace.

TRY IT, YOU MAY LIKE IT

We have tried to share with you some of our common experiences with honesty and sobriety. Firmly convinced that honesty, above everything else, makes it possible for us to apply, or "work," the Twelve Steps of AA, we urge you for recovery's sake with the help of your AA group, your sponsor, or your counselor and fellow patients in a treatment center, to become thoroughly honest not only about your drinking but about your entire life.

For a change in your life, please try honesty. If you have a capacity for honesty, you have a capacity for recovery. And we know you and those you love will benefit from it. At the very least, we assure you it's a relief and a joy to be finally open about ourselves, especially in the company of other recovering people.

Questions for: *Honesty, The Policy of Power*

1. Do you honestly believe you are an alcoholic or drug dependent person? Why?

2. Did you lie about yourself and your life while drinking and using drugs? Describe your behavior.

3. When you were drinking or using drugs, how did you project your own faults and failures upon people close to you?

4. Alcoholics try to live "one day at a time" in pursuit of both

sobriety and an honest way of life. What does the phrase mean to you? How do you intend to apply the saying to your life in the days ahead?

5. How does honesty about your own life make it easier for you to accept other peoples' lives?

6. Recovering alcoholics frequently talk about the necessity of "tough love" in their relationships with each other. What do you think recovering alcoholics mean by the phrase?

3

Cross Addiction, The New Wave

INTRODUCTION

When a human being consumes two or more mood-altering substances in combination, they create a chain reaction within the body, affecting the brain and the entire nervous system. People who use drugs in combination, therefore, become intoxicated much faster and more heavily than people using only one drug. Equally important: they tend to lose control over several drugs in combination much more rapidly than a "mere" alcoholic does with alcohol.

Alcoholics Anonymous was once a fellowship of mostly middle-aged men and women who had finished school, had families and jobs, and drunk alcohol for years, and gradually had lost control over their drinking. Today AA and Narcotics Anonymous are filled with younger persons and some older persons, who may have lost control of several drugs early in life, and never acquired an education, a spouse and family, or even a permanent job.

The author of this chapter is a cross-addicted person recovering in AA. This chapter is directed to all cross-addicted persons—but especially to that group of cross-addicted or polydrug users who are struggling to become sober, self-supporting, and self-respecting persons in adult society.

THE DRUG REVOLUTION

Once upon a time almost all addicts in this country were "pure" alcoholics. They became addicted to one mood-changing drug, ethyl alcohol, which they consumed in common alcoholic beverages.

Nowadays, many addicted persons become dependent on two, three, or more mood-changing drugs at once, though each addict usually has one drug he or she prefers above everything else. Specialists in the treatment of addictions call it their "drug of choice."

The majority of addicts in this country prefer alcohol above all other drugs. Since the development of tranquilizers and the "youth revolution" of the sixties, however, many people have acquired the habit of using other drugs along with alcohol. Many people have drugs of choice other than alcohol, and may become addicted to more than one mood-altering drug. Most Americans who smoke marijuana, for instance, also consume alcohol, and many become addicted to both.

Many addicted people today say that cocaine is their drug of choice. Some people prefer heroin, or similar morphine substitutes such as Demerol—though such users make up only a small percentage of addicted persons. Though they rarely talk about it, some dependent people prefer a tranquilizer like Valium above other drugs, and often consume alcohol along with it. They get intoxicated much faster that way, and become dependent upon both drugs in combination.

And what's wrong with that? Perhaps it's healthy to ingest a variety of mood-changing drugs on an average day. Some people like to think so. Others say: I love the feeling I get from drugs in combination. And whatever feels good is good. Right?

THE NEW WAVE

Wrong. Unfortunately, many gullible people, convinced that whatever feels good is good, drink and drug simultaneously, and end up with terribly serious health problems or perhaps dead.

Many middle-aged drinking people begin using prescribed tranquilizers on a regular basis, and end up addicted. If these people also drink, they frequently become cross-addicted alcoholics.

Under pressure from peers, many naive people drink and drug away their adolescence and become helpless addicts without vocation or family before they are twenty-one.

> *Many middle-aged drinking people*
> *begin using prescribed tranquilizers*
> *on a regular basis, and end up*
> *addicted.*

Often, these younger people smoke marijuana and drink beer in junior high, and a little later pop stimulant or depressant pills, inhale lines of cocaine, and perhaps try LSD. If they get hooked on a combination of alcohol and "street drugs," they tend to lose control over drugs and their bearings in life much faster than the "pure" alcoholics of yesteryear. And there is a reason.

When people of any age use mood-changing drugs in combination, they take very serious chances with multiplying effects within their own systems. They may also be in the process of joining the cross-addicted crowd, the *new wave* of chemically dependent people in this country.

THE PRICE OF CROSS ADDICTION

What happens when people ingest two or more mood-altering drugs into their system?

Unfortunately, when we ingest several drugs affecting our central nervous system at the same time, we mix those drugs together in our bodies and increase the net effect of any one drug. Chemists call the effect "synergistic," or "additive." Addiction specialists say the drugs "potentiate" each other within the body of the user.

Very simply put: alcohol consumed on top of a tranquilizer doubles the effect of either drug taken alone. When I take two similar drugs in combination, I do not add but multiply effects. I double the effect of two drugs and get four times the effect of two.

If I have Valium or marijuana in my system, and pour in alcohol as a mixer, I increase the power of both to affect my moods. If I snort cocaine on top of stimulating medication such as Methedrine, I may get "wired" four times as fast as when I take one or the other by itself. And if I snort cocaine after I get drunk with alcohol, I charge up my nervous system after first shutting it down.

Many cross-addicted people spend their days propelling their nervous systems up and down, depending upon how they feel, and what they have to do during the day or night: alcohol for relaxation in the evening, a pill for sleep, an upper for work, and some more alcohol at noon to cut down on nervousness or anxiety building up during the day.

Often without knowing why, many alcoholics abuse caffeine, nicotine, or mild mood-changing drugs, to bring themselves up, usually in the morning, after an alcoholic binge the day before.

TYPES OF MOOD-ALTERING DRUGS

Mood-changing drugs divide into two basic categories, and then into sub-categories. To change his or her mood by means of drugs, a person may take either a downer or an upper, a depressant or a stimulant.

If he wants to depress feelings of anxiety, he may drink alcohol, far and away the most popular of all mood-changing drugs, or get tranquilizers either from his doctor, or from a dealer on the street or at a party. A doctor will often give a nervous patient Valium or Xanax from the benzodiazepine family of chemicals for tranquilization.

If a person has the sort of anxiety that gives him insomnia, his doctor may give him a sleeping pill such as Dalmane, which in fact has chemical properties similar to Valium. Sleeping pills, however, hypnotize and lethargize the user more soundly than tranquilizers do.

People who visit doctors or purchase drugs off the streets may also obtain barbiturates such as Seconal or Nembutal, or a hypnotic such as Quaaludes, for sleeping purposes. Because these drugs have been widely misused, however, many doctors refuse to prescribe them for outpatients.

When a person uses marijuana, he discovers that a joint or cigarette-length jolt of that drug also takes the edge off his tension— though for most users pot produces "hypnotic" effects somewhat different from the effects of alcohol, and similar to the much more powerful LSD or "acid."

When a person uses heroin or "smack," he discovers that it lowers tension, and anxiety in ways that no other drug does. When heroin addicts take a "fix" of their drug, they feel for a short time as if they have fixed everything in life and death for good. Because they value the effects of heroin so highly, heroin addicts may have greater difficulty recovering than other addicts do.

If a person wants to elevate his or her mood, lose weight, or both, he or she may get from a doctor a stimulant drug such as Dexedrine,

Methedrine or Ritalin, usually called "speed" on the street. If he knows how, he may purchase and use cocaine, the current drug of choice of people who feel they must travel in the "fast lane" of life.

Very simply put: alcohol consumed on top of a tranquilizer doubles the effect of either drug taken alone.

Few doctors today, however, prescribe stimulant medications for weight reduction or even for the relief of fatigue. Doctors have become wary of the danger such drugs create, and rarely prescribe them.

PROBLEMS WITH DEPRESSANTS

The majority of people who take prescribed tranquilizers use them responsibly, and obtain short-term relief from debilitating symptoms of stress and confusion. Since the popular tranquilizers, however, affect the central nervous system roughly the same way alcohol does, a percentage of people become dependent upon them.

Rapidly, these people build up a tolerance or physical need for the drugs, use more than their doctor prescribes, and find themselves regularly intoxicated as a result. In time they discover they can't give the drug up without suffering painful symptoms of withdrawal.

I know. I was once one of those people. I will describe my experiences with depressant chemicals a little later.

PROBLEMS WITH STIMULANTS

Similarly, some people use stimulant medications in a responsible way and obtain short-term relief from severe mental and physical fatigue.

When we use drugs to stimulate our system, however, we may like the effects so much that we use them often and in greater quantities than prescribed or is necessary.

Cocaine or speed addicts tell us they feel so powerful, energetic, and creative when high that they literally never want to come down again. Only when their bodies demand sleep will they allow or force themselves to "crash" in exhaustion. For that reason many "coke" addicts go crazy with confusion brought on in part by severe fatique.

Though most biochemists tell us that stimulants technically do not create a danger of life-threatening withdrawal symptoms, addicted people tell us that stimulants create a psychological and spiritual dependence perhaps more powerful than any the depressant drugs create.

I have heard many persons, cross-addicted to both uppers and downers, say that if they "slipped" and used a drug again, they would use speed rather than alcohol or some other depressant chemical.

> *. . . addicted people become dependent*
> *upon any drugs which alter their*
> *moods, whether up or down, or even*
> *sideways.*

In any case, addicted people may become dependent upon any drugs which alter their moods, whether up or down, or even sideways. Regardless of the variety of mood-altering drugs they use, addicts come to believe they cannot live without those drugs in their systems. Why addicts become so convinced may always remain for them something of a mystery. After years of recovery, many addicts confess they still cannot fully comprehend their previous physical and emotional dependence upon drugs.

A FREE ASSOCIATION QUIZ

Read the statements and write in the blank the first words or answers that honestly come to your mind. Your responses will help you discover to what degree you depend upon the effects of alcohol and other drugs for your social life.

1. I drink alcohol and use other drugs at least occasionally. The other drugs are _____.

2. When I smoke marijuana and drink alcohol, I feel _____.

3. When a friend suggests that I go with him or her to get drunk or stoned, I feel _____.

4. People who always drink and often use other drugs to have

fun are real _____ (winners, losers, or what?).

5. When I am drinking and using drugs around other people, my sexual instincts are _____ (dampened, aroused, or what?).

6. After a heavy night of partying, the next morning I feel

_____.

7. When I see other people drunk or stoned I feel _____.

8. After the first drink, joint, pill, or line of cocaine, I feel like stopping? _____ Having some more? _____ Getting drunk or stoned? _____. (Check one.)

If you respond affirmatively to three of questions 2-7, you probably depend heavily upon drugs to have a "good time." People who use drugs in order to have fun are very frequently addicted to those drugs.

THE ILLNESS OF ADDICTION—A PERSONAL HISTORY

Addicts become profoundly and fatally ill.

Please note for starters: drug users do not "decide" to become dependent upon drugs and thus use more than the doctor prescribes, or they buy on the streets. They lose control over drug use exactly the way an alcoholic loses control over the use of alcohol. The user can't make his willpower work against his feeling of need for the effects his drug produces.

An addict's drug acts like a foreign agent within his body, which, ironically, he feels he needs for continuing existence. Because he can no longer control the use of a drug, the addict becomes a person sick in mind, body, and spirit.

When I injured my back 20 years ago, a well-meaning orthopedic doctor prescribed Seconal, a barbiturate medication, to help me sleep in the midst of steady and often severe pain. Though prior to the injury I often drank beer on a social basis, I did not think to tell the doctor about it. And he asked me nothing about my drinking habits.

About six months later, however, I found myself regularly drinking more beer and using more Seconal than before—more beer, in fact, than I had ever consumed in my life. My intake literally went up from an average of maybe one 12-ounce bottle every few days to two quart bottles in an evening! Without openly telling my doctor, I also doubled my intake of sleeping pills.

As time went on, I found myself fat, perpetually sleepy, unsteady on my feet, and prone to memory lapses. I would make a telephone call in the evening and forget in the morning what I said—or whom I called. Occasionally, I forgot that I had made the call altogether. Later I learned that I had experienced a "blackout," a memory loss.

Sometimes I drank at odd hours of the afternoon, jeopardizing both my job and my relationship with my long-suffering wife. For the first time in my life, I hid a bottle of hard liquor from my wife—gin, I think it was—in an old shoe in the closet. When I had a really bad case of insomnia, I would nip at the bottle in the shoe to put myself back to sleep.

I became convinced I was crazy, and went to a psychiatrist, who more or less agreed with me. He also gave me more Seconal and a tranquilizer as a chaser. By the end of two years, my back pain began to subside, but my "insomnia," my depression, and anxiety still raged fiercely. By then I had come to believe I could not exist without my tranquilizers—though I had not had a "downer" in pill form until I was thirty-two years old.

After moving to a new city, therefore, I searched out yet another psychiatrist who diagnosed me "depressive," and gave me a veritable smorgasbord of mood-altering pills. I kept on taking pills for about five years until I finally landed in a treatment center for alcoholism and drug addiction.

At no time during that period did any doctor tell me I should not drink while taking those mood-altering medications. At no time did any doctor suggest to me that I might be addicted to those medications and alcohol in combination.

By the time I entered treatment, however, I could have as easily jumped over the moon as broken my drug habit by myself. I had become desperately ill from the use of depressant chemicals. To keep on living, I needed immediate help from people specializing in the treatment of cross addiction—simultaneous addiction to alcohol and other drugs.

In treatment, I learned some hard facts about cross addiction. For starters, I discovered that withdrawal from alcohol and tranquilizers is more than twice as difficult as withdrawal from plain, old alcohol.

COMPLICATIONS FROM COMBINATIONS

When addicted persons use alcohol and other mood-altering drugs together, they complicate withdrawal and abstinence from those drugs.

Most alcoholics can withdraw from alcohol in about 48-72 hours. In that time, their body eliminates all alcohol from the tissues, and leaves it relatively free from withdrawal pains such as stomach and muscle cramps, headaches, nervousness, insomnia and seizures.

If, however, the addicted person uses both alcohol and tranquilizers in combination, he or she faces a somewhat more complicated problem of withdrawal. Unfortunately, the body does not eliminate tranquilizers as quickly as it eliminates alcohol.

If I take five or ten milligrams of Valium on a given day, I will gradually eliminate that amount from my system in about 20 hours. If I take Valium or Dalmane to go to sleep, I will wake up with about half the amount still in my system, and need the better part of the day to eliminate it completely.

But when I take larger amounts of Valium or Dalmane on a daily basis over a long period of time, my body simply cannot eliminate the chemicals completely in one day. Instead, my body stores the chemicals in fat tissue and tries to get rid of them as fast as it can, given the machinery it has to work with. The steady and heavy tranquilizer user, in other words, becomes a walking storehouse of his drug of choice.

In fact, when we tranquilizer addicts try to withdraw from our drug, we need at least ten days to rid ourselves of the greater portion of the drug in our system. For the first few days we may think we're in good shape, because we're still drawing on drug reserves in our body tissues. By the tenth day, however, when our system finally gets rid of most of the traces, we may go bananas and can even have a seizure. Fortunately, in a treatment center, seizures during withdrawal by depressant drugs can be prevented by appropriate medication.

As odd and unfair as it may seem, withdrawal from tranquilizers and most sleeping pills takes longer than withdrawal from any other drug, including heroin. Many treatment specialists believe that heavy drug users may eliminate all traces of depressant chemicals from their systems only after six months or more of abstinence. In the long run, however, abstinence from tranquilizing drugs can be carried out as successfully as abstinence from alcohol, or other mood-altering drugs.

ONE FOR ALL

Finally, to the most complicated and controversial issue of all: most doctors specializing in addictive disorders believe addicts who become dependent upon one mood-altering drug become, even without using them, dependent upon all mood-altering drugs. Since I am an alcoholic, I am technically susceptible also to heroin, marijuana, cocaine, LSD, nicotine, narcotic pain-killers, tranquilizers, sleeping pills, and all commodities such as cough syrups and decongestants containing any chemicals which may alter my mood by even a smidgeon.

Though I may prefer alcohol and find myself peculiarly susceptible to abuse of it, I will find it impossible to use without abusing the other addictive chemicals as well. It's a melancholy and even frightening thought, but, I believe, basically accurate.

Many alcoholics, for instance, use Valium to alleviate nervous symptoms created at least in part by alcohol. If they tell you, "I drink too much, but don't abuse Valium," they may tell the truth, but only in part. Actually, they feed their bodies the same kinds of chemicals, one in liquid and one in solid form.

Alcoholics often "prove" to themselves the close relationship between depressant chemicals by abstaining from alcohol and substituting a tranquilizing drug. When alcoholics do so, however, the majority then proceed to abuse the tranquilizer—use more than prescribed—because of their general tolerance for all depressant chemicals.

When alcoholics substitute tranquilizers for alcohol, they also may "set themselves up" for a slip into their preferred drug, alcohol. Similarly, when alcoholics try to substitute marijuana for alcohol, they make themselves vulnerable to another drink.

Now, we are not suggesting that addicts move, as on "steppingstones," from pot to alcohol to heroin, or something similar. No one drug leads automatically to any other drug. The vast majority of marijuana smokers, for instance, do not move on to heroin. Rather, any person who lowers his inhibitions by intoxication through one drug makes himself susceptible to the desire for another.

> *. . . addicted people are prone to dependency on all mood-altering drugs for the rest of their lives.*

The melancholy truth is: addicted people are prone to dependency on all mood-altering drugs for the rest of their lives. They must, in fact, try to be frank and truthful with their own doctors, so as to avoid consuming, except in real emergencies, any addictive drugs.

THE TOUGH BUT HAPPY TRUTH ABOUT RECOVERY

The road to recovery may be tougher for cross-addicted persons. Withdrawal takes time and courage. And since pills don't create breath odor, they pose special temptations for relapse to all addicts.

And unfortunately, many younger addicts of our acquaintance have paid a price-tag peculiar to their generation. Whereas we older alcoholics usually enter AA with some adult experience and perspective, with jobs, and spouses who may out of love or necessity have stuck with us, many younger addicts enter AA without significant drug-free experiences at all. Since they pursued relationships and "goals" by means of drugs, they must learn from scratch how to function as mature adults without drugs.

To create one's self in one's late teens, or twenties, out of nothing, seems impossible to younger addicts. And it is. In AA, however, many young members learn the same lesson we older alcoholics learned from the founders of our fellowship: we gain the power of recovery only when we realize that we have no power of our own to recover. As we come to believe powers greater than ourselves—our God, our AA group, and other people—can restore us to spiritual, emotional and physical health, we have a chance for recovery.

The happy truth is: cross-addicted persons may recover from dependency by following the AA steps of recovery. No matter what the causes of addiction, the beginning of recovery is always just two honest statements away: "We admitted that we were powerless over alcohol, or any other mood-altering drug—and we came to believe that a Power greater than ourselves could restore us to sanity."

Many addicted young people are recovering in AA or NA today because they have entered treatment and reached out for help from other recovering addicts.

So long as we retain the great Twelve Steps of AA or any other fellowship using the Twelve Steps, we cross-addicted people, young and older, may look forward to renewed self-confidence, a growing spirituality, a new and meaningful way of life, love, and a kind of comradeship in recovery scarcely available to non-addicted people. That possibility is supremely worth living for.

Questions for: *Cross Addiction, The New Wave*

    1. When a person uses two mood-altering drugs, such as alcohol and Valium, on the same day, those drugs "potentiate," or of-

ten double in power within the body. What experience have you had with multiple drug use?

2. If you have abused stimulant drugs, such as cocaine, Methedrine or Dexedrine, or even too much coffee, describe the effects upon your nervous system.

3. If you have used uppers, such as cocaine or speed to wake up and stay awake, and downers, such as alcohol or tranquilizers, to relax or go to sleep, describe the effects upon your nervous system.

4. Have you become dependent upon mood-altering drugs you received from your doctor? How did this happen? Describe your experiences.

5. If your drug of choice is alcohol, why do you think marijuana or any other mood-altering drug, would be dangerous for you to use?

6. If you have abused drugs from the time of your adolescence or your teenage years, how do you plan to rebuild your life and attain mature adulthood?

4

Killer Cocaine

INTRODUCTION

Cocaine is a stimulant which has been cultivated and used since time immemorial by people in several South American countries. Europeans and Americans have been aware of cocaine since the Spanish conquests of the Americas in the 16th century. Recognizing the dangers of cocaine abuse, the United States and other countries passed laws to ban the drug from the marketplace early in the 20th century.

In the 1960's, however, "entrepreneurs" in various countries discovered ways to buy, process, and sell cocaine illegally in potent forms for recreational use. Overnight, cocaine became the "in drug," first of the rich, and then of a variety of groups across the land. As a powerful stimulant, cocaine came to match the dominating theme of the '80's perfectly: the need to succeed at all costs in life and love, work and play.

In the '80's, however, the world also discovered, as if for the first time, that cocaine is a dangerously habit-forming drug, terribly destructive to both body and mind. Cocaine, the in drug, became cocaine, the killer of body and mind.

This chapter describes some of the history of cocaine use and abuse. Through the stories of recovering addicts, it also offers hope to people or families who find themselves presently overwhelmed by the threat of cocaine dependence.

IT BEGAN WITH THE INCAS

When the Spanish *conquistadors* first encountered the Inca empire in the sixteenth century, they found that the emperor himself controlled the use of a remarkable drug contained in the leaves of a mountain shrub now called, technically, *Erthroxylon coca.* Inca people who chewed the leaves of the coca plant experienced euphoria, bursts of energy, the illusion of power, and even immortality. The Incas, in fact, utilized coca leaves heavily in common worship. On the verge of death, people with the leaves in their mouths were thought to go immediately to paradise.

Though wary for religious reasons of using the drug themselves, the conquering Spaniards controlled the supply of the substance among the Indians, while realizing a considerable profit in sales. They became, thereby, a type of the first cocaine "pusher" in history.

High in the Andes Mountains, where the coca shrub has been cultivated and used for centuries, South American Indians still chew the leaves daily, and seem to experience few dangerous side effects— perhaps because they use the drug in an unrefined, and hence mild form, as a means of survival in their harsh mountain environment.

IN EUROPE AND AMERICA

In the nineteenth century, European and American scientists, medical doctors, and well-known artists, developed a deep interest in cocaine. Sigmund Freud experimented widely with cocaine extract both upon himself and others, and at first thought it was a "miracle" antidote for depression, fatigue, and even morphine addiction. Only after one of his addicted friends and patients became dependent upon cocaine, did Freud come to realize its dangers, and decide quietly to give up the use of it himself.

In America, the famous medical doctor, William Halsted, of Johns Hopkins University, became addicted to both cocaine and morphine, and even after strenuous efforts over a lifetime was unsuccessful in arresting his habit.

Although before the 1960's Europeans and Americans rarely used cocaine extract in pure form, they did in the 19th century introduce cocaine into various drinks and patent medicines, including Mariana's wine in Europe, and liver pills, cough syrups, and Coca-Cola in America. Thomas Edison, President William McKinley, and the novelist, Jules Verne, all praised Mariana's wine publicly. Verne said, "A single bottle of Mariana's extraordinary coca wine guarantees a lifetime of a hundred years." In a message of January 2, 1898, Pope Leo XIII gave Mr. Mariani a gold medal for the invention of his famous wine and cocaine mix. Only under pressure from the new federal Pure Food and Drug Act of 1906, did the American Coca-Cola Company substitute the milder stimulant, caffeine, for cocaine in their products.

Many drug historians believe that at the turn of the century thousands of Americans and Europeans unwittingly became addicted to cocaine in a variety of liquid forms, but were unable to find persons competent to diagnose their condition. In fact, recognition and understanding of the nature of cocaine addiction has come very slowly in America and in Europe.

THE LURE OF THE MASTER STIMULANT

Since the time of the Harrison Narcotic Act of 1914, cocaine has been mistakenly classified in America as a narcotic and been subjected to the same laws affecting opium, morphine, and heroin. In fact, cocaine is a powerful stimulant, and produces effects similar to the much-publicized "speed," or amphetamine drugs. Many experts believe cocaine has literally replaced amphetamines as the addict's stimulant "drug of choice."

Why are so many people in America presently attracted to a stimulant drug such as cocaine? Why do we face a veritable "epidemic" of cocaine abuse in the United States in the 1980's? Just at the time when marijuana use seems on the decline?

If you simply consider for a moment your own desire or need for caffeine in coffee, tea, or cola products, you will begin already to realize why some people are drawn to much more powerful stimulants. If you have trouble starting or continuing your day without cups of coffee, you know why millions of persons in the world have come to value the effects of cocaine almost beyond the price of gold itself.

"With cocaine you are industructible, perfect, the giant of your dreams."

If, furthermore, you feel at all driven by your family members, your peers, or by advertisements to succeed at all costs in school, work, and other relationships, you can easily grasp why so many Americans, constantly stimulated by these forces, would fall back upon a stimulant drug to provide both the energy for and the illusion of perceived success. You can begin to understand why the illegal sale of cocaine in the world has become a multi-billion dollar "industry."

Researchers have proven conclusively that stimulant drugs give the user a physical and mental lift. When you feel fatigue lift and your brain "turn on" and lock into position for work after that first cup of coffee, you have not experienced an illusion. When used in moderation, stimulant drugs do wake you up, improve your mental capabilities, and make you feel more capable of accomplishing your work or play.

Unfortunately, cocaine can accomplish far more than caffeine and much faster. As people learn how to use cocaine, they can in a matter of minutes after inhaling, smoking, or injecting the drug give themselves a feeling of intense euphoria, high energy, boundless optimism, and the illusion they can accomplish any goal and fulfill any dream they have, with a minimum of effort.

According to Verteel Pendelton, a Chicago drug-abuse specialist and former user, quoted in *The Coke Book*, "With cocaine you are indestructible, perfect, the giant of your dreams." Another former user quoted in the same book says, "Cocaine is ego food. It feeds the ego like nothing I've ever seen."*

With results such as these, any person could be tempted to use cocaine. Unfortunately, we believe the drug is peculiarly tempting to Americans. Some recovering addicts we know call it the Great American Dream Drug, and there is a reason. It seems to fit American needs, most particularly of those American young people who consider themselves upwardly mobile.

ARE YOU VULNERABLE TO COCAINE USE AND ABUSE?

1. Do you frequently feel down and wish you could quickly put yourself into an up mood?

2. Do you place a high value on the feeling of euphoria? On feeling as if you were the center of everyone's attention?

3. Do you often feel worn out or tired, even upon waking in the morning, and feel the need for a stimulant to get you going?

*From *The Coke Book*, a Berkley Book. Used by permission.

4. When you see other people having "fun" with cocaine, do you feel the need to experience the same fun?

5. Do you feel insecure about sex and relationships, and wish you could raise your self-confidence by use of a drug?

6. Have you ever thought of using cocaine just to get through a day at work?

7. Do you use cocaine to raise your confidence and be a success at work or in social situations?

8. Have you driven a car while under the influence of cocaine?

These questions will help you decide whether you have the potential for addiction to cocaine. If you find yourself saying yes to more than a few, you may be on your way to addiction. Perhaps you have already arrived.

USING COCAINE—SNORTING

Some of us first used cocaine under a little pressure from friends at a party. We became involved in what some experts call a "cocaine ceremony," almost a variety of religious experience providing status to both provider and user.

Our host literally laid out "lines of snow," or coke crystals, with a razor blade on a long, glass coffee table in his living room. Because he had a good salary, he supplied us with glass straws, or little spoons if we preferred, by which we could snuff the crystals up our nostrils. Later we learned to snort coke with rolled dollar bills, or twenties, or hundreds, if we had them, to prove our status and superiority.

When a person "snorts" coke, he or she first experiences a numbing sensation in the nose, or on any other surface, such as the gums or genitals, where the substance is applied. Cocaine is a "topical anesthetic," and numbs whatever body tissue it contacts. Some people we've known have applied coke to the penis or clitoris, in an attempt to numb sexual feelings and prolong intercourse.

As the cocaine crystals enter the nose, they dissolve on the walls of the mucous membranes and are absorbed into the bloodstream. The blood quickly carries the drug to the brain and in sufficient amounts produces an immediate sensation of euphoria and energy. The drug also produces a stuffy nose and bad sinuses. Jokes about bad sinuses are legion among cocaine users.

When used in moderation (not unlike alcohol), cocaine seems to serve as an aphrodisiac for both men and women indulging in intercourse—perhaps because it frees a person from inhibitions and initially increases confidence in personal powers.

Those of us who continued to use cocaine on a regular basis enjoyed the euphoria created by the drug, but also wanted to build up a sense of confidence, to be a success in life. The reason for cocaine use is almost that simple. On a moderate dose of cocaine, it is virtually impossible to feel negative about anything. The drug convinces a person that he will do well in whatever he engages, that everything will turn out well for him in the future. The feeling is intoxicating and very hard to duplicate without the drug.

Those of us who continued to use
cocaine . . . wanted to build up a sense
of confidence to be a success in life.

FREE-BASING COCAINE

When people use cocaine over a period of time and build up a tolerance for it—a need for more coke to produce the desired effects—they will often turn to smoking either coca as a paste, or as free-base.

Free-base smoking is a popular form of recreational cocaine use in the United States. In fact, users may now purchase prepackaged free-base kits to engage in what can be a highly dangerous form of cocaine ingestion. Free-base is created by treating street cocaine with chemicals, some of which are flammable. In the process of preparing and smoking the extract, the user runs a high risk of setting himself on fire.

CRACK

Crack is an even more concentrated form of cocaine, easily and cheaply produced, and sold on the streets in small crystals or chunks which can be smoked. Because of crack's quick and potent effect on the nervous system, users tend to become rapidly dependent upon the high it produces. Since the effects of crack are very transient, however, users also find they must smoke it repeatedly, as often as every half hour, to reproduce the effect. Tolerance for this form of the drug, therefore, usually develops more rapidly than with any other forms of cocaine.

EFFECTS

When smoking free-base or crack, a user experiences a sudden, intense rush of energy, accompanied by dilated pupils, rapid heart rate, increased blood pressure, and fast breathing. Most of us also experience an illusion of power and competence difficult to put into words. Unfortunately, the high lasts only about 15 to 30 minutes, and then subsides into a feeling of restless irritability. Sleep is virtually impossible for anyone who is binging on free-base. For that reason, many of us have turned to alcohol, other depressant drugs, or even heroin, in order to come down from a high for sleep.

A few of us have injected heroin and cocaine simultaneously—the "speedball" made famous by the late John Belushi—in order to moderate the severe low we experience as the cocaine begins to wear off in our systems.

PATHOLOGICAL REACTIONS

What came next for us is painful to remember and describe. If we could have used cocaine "socially" or moderately for the rest of our lives, we would probably have done it. So powerful is the euphoria produced by the stimulant that we still have difficulty imagining life without that high.

In fact, for many years some of us were convinced by faulty studies done with cocaine users that cocaine addiction was technically impossible since the user experienced few severe physical withdrawal symptoms, such as seizures, when giving up the drug.

Unfortunately, we did discover after regular use at parties and other social affairs, that we swiftly built up an inward need to maintain that high feeling of euphoria and energy as long as possible by using more and more of the drug. Soon, we began to use cocaine privately to meet the challenges of our work, of sex, and our everyday living.

We tried to tell ourselves, in the language of drug research, that we were becoming "psychologically" rather than physically dependent upon or addicted to cocaine. But we became quite simply addicted. Our nervous system demanded more and more cocaine. Many of us found that we could attempt no task of any complexity or magnitude, particularly connected with our job or work, *without* the prior use of cocaine.

Since one does not become "drunk" on cocaine, but rather high and "wired," it is difficult to make comparisons between abusive cocaine and alcohol ingestion. An alcoholic will finally pass out after he or she has consumed a sufficient quantity of alcohol. A cocaine addict becomes highly irritable, anxious, and even paranoid when he or she has consumed a great deal of cocaine over an extended period of time, but feels *in a conscious* state an absolutely compulsive need for more of the drug.

> *Many of us found that we could*
> *attempt no task of any complexity or*
> *magnitude . . . without the prior use*
> *of cocaine.*

The feeling is difficult to describe. We have, for instance, when highly wired after days of cocaine use, felt when we ran out of the drug, as if we were literally going to crack. We have hit the streets looking for a drug source, and found ourselves in a state of absolute and abject fear and panic. We have walked down a sidewalk and felt that every person we saw was going to mug or kill us, that all humanity had turned against us, that we could no longer hang on to our sanity, let alone fulfill the dreams we experienced under the influence of cocaine.

One of us vividly remembers experiencing a severe anxiety reaction on the streets of New York, and upon impulse, walking into a recruiting station and enlisting in the U.S. Navy. Why? To come down from a high and avoid, at least temporarily, further use of cocaine. When on duty aboard ship in the navy, we thought it would be tough to snort cocaine on a regular basis.

One of us vividly remembers using up all the supply he had planned to sell on the streets to other users, hitting the streets trying unsuccessfully to borrow money to buy more cocaine, and coming back to hide in a bedroom closet for protection against enemies and attackers, human, animal, and insect. A few of us have, after such terrifying experiences, made the decision almost on the spur of the moment to seek help from others—and ultimately from a treatment center.

THE COCAINE PREDICAMENT

We feel that cocaine addiction is more difficult to break than addiction to depressant drugs such as alcohol. Interestingly enough, studies conducted both in Los Angeles and in Washington, D.C., in which apes and monkeys were given unlimited supplies of cocaine, indicated that the addicted subjects preferred cocaine to food, sex, or *any other drug*.

The cocaine addict cannot even fall into a protective sleep between binges. He or she has to keep going, or drift into a state of panicky helplessness and hopelessness. Meanwhile, as the user keeps snorting or perhaps injecting the drug he becomes so anxious, jumpy, and uncoordinated physically and mentally, that he literally can't function any longer on or off the drug.

To "crash" or fall asleep the addict may use a depressive or narcotic drug. After he wakes or comes to, however, he feels an immediate and overwhelmingly compulsive need for more cocaine to regain his sense of confidence and power.

To make things more difficult, the coke addict must always purchase drugs illegally from friends or from pushers off the streets or in housing projects of the major cities. As he becomes more and more dependent upon more and more cocaine, he will, unless he has unlimited sources of money, begin to cut his own supply with chemicals and sell it to friends, or in desperation, on the streets.

Many cocaine addicts, especially those who are young and not yet established in jobs with a reasonable income, become coke pushers. Others choose to do so simply for the fantastic profits that can be made from illegal coke sales on the open market. Like the heroin addict, the coke user may be forced to steal to get drugs. Like heroin addicts, some cocaine users in this country end up giving sex away to a dealer in order to maintain a high.

In such a state of mind, the cocaine addict is completely unpredictable. He or she may cry one moment and burst into a towering and physically abusive rage in the next. He or she may alternate between abject demands for help and pity, and grotesque attempts at manipulation or domination of others.

Nothing works any longer for the addict or those who try to deal with him. The addict loses his ability to make realistic decisions, his attention span, memory, motor coordination, sense of decency toward others, and responsibility toward the most elementary tasks and relationships. Even the most sympathetic and experienced people find it impossible either to work with or relate to cocaine addicts wired on their drug.

Since the addict feels, however, that he will go promptly crazy without his drug—and his friends may feel so also—no one knows exactly what to do. If he withdraws briefly from cocaine use, he usually experiences such deep depression, accompanied by horrible guilt, self-loathing, and conviction of failure, that he turns back to cocaine for what seems to him to be survival itself.

WHO USES COCAINE?

Whereas cocaine was once considered the Rolls Royce of the drug scene, a glamour drug literally beyond the price of all but the richest people, vast supplies from South America have in recent years brought the price of coke down into the middle and even the lower economic classes of American society.

Most Americans, of course, have read of the problems famous athletes and entertainers have had with cocaine. The deaths of people such as John Belushi, Freddie Prinz, and Len Bias, and the severe problems of people such as the actress Mackenzie Phillips, and sports stars John Lucas and Mercury Morris, have become legendary in our time. In our experience, however, not only the famous and wealthy use cocaine. Most younger poly-addicted persons we know, rich or not, have used cocaine along with other drugs, usually alcohol, marijuana, or pills.

Futhermore, while we were using cocaine, we met persons with all sorts of jobs—young business people, lawyers, professors and students, accountants, mechanics, secretaries, assembly line workers, flight attendants—and heard of entertainers of all kinds, athletes, physicians, airline pilots, and investment brokers who used cocaine, and often sold it regularly for a profit.

. . . while we were using cocaine, we
met persons with all sorts of jobs . . .
who used cocaine, and often sold it . . .

Most of these people begin to use cocaine not only to have "fun," to enhance music and the sex drive, or to get high at a social affair, but also to stay awake and alert on the job. Many athletes firmly believe cocaine enhances their performance. So also entertainers, sales and business people in high-pressure positions may believe that the drug not only keeps them awake but makes them sharper, mentally quicker, and more alert.

On the other end of the spectrum, people in tedious jobs may choose to use cocaine simply to avoid fatigue and endless boredom. Using cocaine can seem like salvation itself to an assembly line or clerical worker doomed to do the same task incessantly week in and week out.

To abstain from cocaine you will need a supportive community where you can share your recovery experience . . .

A former California Congressman has admitted to spending $100,000 on cocaine while representing his district in Washington. Cocaine use among physicians is thought to be higher than among any other professinal group, not only because of the high-pressure nature of the job, but because of plentiful and available supply.

Accessibility to more reasonably priced cocaine is surely one of the reasons that so many more Americans and Europeans use the drug today. We believe, however, that the high premium placed upon vocational and financial success also plays a role in cocaine use. If you want to succeed in life at all costs, you will not abuse alcohol, marijuana, or LSD, for fear that these depressant or hallucinatory drugs will hold you back. Rather you will take the optimum stimulant drug to give you a feeling of supreme confidence while you pursue your dreams.

Unfortunately, and for many of us tragically, we succeeded instead in becoming hopelessly addicted to a drug which rendered us helpless, unable to sleep, eat, exercise, have sex, relate to others, or even do our work. Whereas we began using cocaine to have fun, we ended up on the streets looking daily for a fix of coke just to get over the massive depression we experienced in withdrawal from coke.

We ended up using cocaine in order to prevent the symptoms of cocaine use. It is a familiar predicament for all addicts, no matter what the addictive substance. For us it was the beginning of an end, which was also the beginning of a new life without coke or any other mood-altering drugs.

BEGINNING RECOVERY

We cocaine addicts have, by ourselves, found no way out of the dilemma of addiction. This simple fact has primary significance for any coke addict seeking relief and recovery. You can't do it by yourself.

Not only will you experience too much panic and anxiety in withdrawal to persist on your own, you will find even if you emerge successfully from acute anxiety or perhaps a psychotic reaction to withdrawal, that you will not be able to stay off coke without treatment. To abstain from cocaine you will need a supportive community where you can share your recovery experience with other recovering addicts.

If this sounds to you suspiciously like Alcoholics Anonymous talk, you are right. It is. Most of us have discovered through treatment, in AA, NA, or CA, that the Twelve Step program of recovery works well for cocaine addiction and dependence upon any other drugs to which we may have become accustomed.

The renowned expert on cocaine addiction, treatment and recovery, Dr. David E. Smith, subscribes to a variation of the AA program which he calls the "Science of Art" method of treatment, A standing for "acceptance," R for "reduction of stimulation," and T for "talkdown."

In the acceptance phase, we recovering coke addicts came to accept our powerlessness over and total dependence upon cocaine for existence. In the process, however, we also came to accept cocaine abuse as an illness to which we did not have to attach social stigma.

To reduce our need for artificial stimulation by cocaine or any other stimulant drug, most of us found it necessary to enter a treatment program—usually one connected with a treatment center for alcoholism and other forms of drug abuse. There we found the kind of quiet and supportive environment we needed to get through depressive reactions to withdrawal, and gradually to learn how to function day by day without resorting to coke for stimulation.

Fortunately for cocaine addicts,
dozens of excellent treatment centers
have programs tailored to cocaine . . .

Finally, we discovered in treatment and afterwards in AA, NA or CA, or in other cocaine recovery groups where all members have experienced cocaine addiction, how to continue recovery happily and peacefully.

Fortunately for cocaine addicts, dozens of excellent treatment centers now have programs tailored to cocaine and amphetamine addiction. The possibility of recovery for you or for your loved ones is probably just a phone call away. If you cannot find in your white or yellow pages any centers specifically treating cocaine addiction, we suggest you call one or more of your local alcoholism treatment centers and ask for information. If you cannot reach a center, you may simply call your local AA number and ask where a cocaine user might find information and help.

HOPE FOR THE FUTURE

If statisticians claim that there are now millions of coke abusers in this country, we may claim that there are also thousands of cocaine addicts presently free from drugs, stable, and recovering with the help of a supportive group, a program, and for many of us, a God of our understanding whom we believe literally has helped us back from insanity and possible death from addiction.

Cocaine addiction is deadly business. If the user does not kill himself by overdosing, or through a heart attack, he may destroy his sanity, jeopardize his legal freedom, lose his job, family, and friends, and join the dregs of society in endless pursuit of his drug. Before seeking help, many of us have found ourselves in such profoundly degrading social circumstances that we do not care even to describe them in print.

When we finally admitted to a caring person that we needed help, however, we found our way into treatment. We found our way into recovery groups which provided us weekly insight into our illness, impetus for well being, and also wonderful social relationships of a kind we never really had when we were using and abusing drugs.

If you are presently at the end of your rope with your own addiction, or with the addiction of a friend or family member, pick up your phone. Help may be just one word away for you. There is life beyond coke. Cocaine is a killer for many. But it has been for us an entrance into a new way of life much better than we ever dreamed possible when we were high and wired.

Questions for: *Killer Coke*

1. If you have used cocaine, describe your first experience with it.

2. A former cocaine addict has called cocaine "ego food." What do you think he means by the phrase?

3. What effects of cocaine caused you the most discomfort or difficulty?

4. Why do you think cocaine addicts in withdrawal often think they are going crazy or even experience genuine psychotic episodes?

5. A person addicted to cocaine and seeking help must first admit he or she has lost control over its use. Why do you think that is true?

6. Why do you think a continuing support group such as AA, NA, or CA is necessary for continuing abstinence and recovery from cocaine addiction?

5

Tough on Women

INTRODUCTION

Since the beginning of human history and the first stories of human drunkenness, society seems to have been "tougher" on female than on male drinkers. People have more easily accepted the consumption of alcohol, and other mood-altering drugs, among men than among women. As a result, society has historically been more condemning of drunken and alcoholic women than drunken and alcoholic men.

The writer of this chapter, an older recovering alcoholic woman, describes how the attitudes of society and her family members contributed to her problems, but also helped to make treatment and recovery in Alcoholics Anonymous possible for her.

The chapter will help any woman concerned about her drinking and drug use. It may also prove helpful for family members or friends who love her and want to help her back to sobriety and good health.

MY STORY

I am an old-fashioned alcoholic woman. By that I mean that I have always been a housewife. I have a loving husband, three children, and seven grandchildren, and did all of my heavy drinking at home—"in the closet," as we say nowadays. I have never in my life had a drink alone in a bar or any other public setting. Outside of my own home, I don't think I have ever been drunk.

Though it sounds funny now, I am not sure I ever got drunk before I was fifty-four. By the time I was 55, and my last son was off to college,

I was drunk every day without fail. Whereas I could not previously finish even a moderately-sized glass of light wine during the duration of a long meal, now I could polish off a whole bottle of any sort of wine in less than five minutes, and for several years did so each morning to start the day.

Frequently, I timed myself and took perverse satisfaction in my ability to get the wine down fast. I could get drunk so much faster if I drank quickly, especially on an empty stomach.

Because my husband was still active as an officer in our family business and often worked six days and even evenings per week, I drank mostly alone to overcome what I thought were symptoms of depression. In my own mind, I seemed only to be medicating myself, and for very good reason. I felt genuinely lonely and sorry for myself. My husband still had his work, and I was in menopause and had lost my children forever.

---

*Only when I was drunk did I feel
really at ease and "myself."*

Only when I was drunk did I feel really at ease and "myself." Only when I was drunk did the universe itself seem to fall into place. Those hundreds of bottles of white wine seemed, I think, to replace my children whom I missed so much, replaced the sound of their gossip and laughter, even their bickering and angry arguments.

When we had occasional parties at our home, I was now the drunken "life of the party." I made, served, and drank most of the drinks. I was the one my friends gossiped about, and chose in time to ignore. And when they chose to ignore me, I ignored them right back. When they refused to invite me to their parties, I promptly dropped them from my list. One by one, I dropped all my friends from my list, and settled down with my one friend, my bottle.

THE OLD-FASHIONED PATTERN

Among women my age in recovery from alcoholism, my pattern of drinking is a familiar one. Though we realize now we had no excuse for drinking, let alone losing control of our drinking, we thought when our children left for college or got married, that we needed alcohol to get rid of the blues. We needed alcohol and those lovely tranquilizers from our doctor to cope with the "empty nest syndrome." We needed alcohol and pills to cope with a husband who seemed suddenly absorbed in his work, and perhaps even running around with younger women from his office, we thought.

Toward the end of my drinking career the "empty nest syndrome" became my favorite phrase. Whenever my husband cautioned, lectured, or berated me over my daily drunkenness, I would rattle on about menopause and the empty nest syndrome. And because my husband is, I think, an unusually kind, generous and loving man, he sympathized with me.

To this day, I have no idea how he put up with all of this, except for the pure love of me, and for the God we share, for which I shall always be grateful. Without my husband, I would surely be dead or on the "wrong" side of the door in a mental institution.

It was pure hell, but not for the reasons I gave to my husband. After a year or so of drinking to get rid of the blues, I no longer thought much about my children, or even of the blues. I have no way of describing or explaining this feeling. All I thought about was my next drink. I seemed no longer to care about my children or myself.

I drank in the morning to get rid of the shakes produced by my intake of the day before. I drank in the afternoon to get rid of the gathering hangover from my morning's drinking. I drank at night, especially when my husband was at home, to get rid of the horrible fear and guilt I felt over my inability to stop drinking at all. And when occasionally I abstained from alcohol for a day, I binged on sweets, especially chocolate chip cookies, which became my favorite replacement for alcohol.

During the day I watched soap operas and often browsed trashy romance novels of the type you can buy off racks at supermarkets. My reasons for watching and reading, however, had little to do, I think, with sex. Basically, I read and watched to discover "nice" people who seemed worse off than I was: people fearful and disheveled, in and out of beds and bars and sanitariums, and constantly drinking like I did. Somehow it seemed to me that if they did it, that justified my doing it, even though they were figments of someone's fevered imagination.

Though I did not realize it fully, I had lost control over my emotions, my thoughts, my drinking, and myself. I had turned my will and life over to the carefully hidden bottle of chablis I downed promptly every morning after my husband left for his office. Though I could claim to be alive, I was really quite dead inside. Alcohol had taken me over and left me no more self-control than a one-year-old child.

I would have kept drinking the rest of my life, had not my loving husband and children gotten together and decided to hustle me off into a treatment center. Like Betty Ford's family members confronted her, mine confronted me through an "intervention." And though I hated their words, and thought them loveless and spiteful, and above all lacking all understanding of my precious depression, I could not deny the truth of the confrontation.

They called me a drunk and proved it by reminding me of dozens of drunken evenings, mornings, afternoons, of hidden bottles, pills in my purse, in my clothes, in coffee cans, of spilled drinks, slurred words, conversations blacked out, of failures to buy food, cook meals, clean clothes, wash my face, comb my hair, of sleeping on the living room floor, of sleeping on the cold basement floor for hours one evening, something I'll never quite remember, and in a fit of drunken rage killing our cat with a spatula, which I don't really care to go into.

They gave it to me straight, and I could not swallow the truth. But since I could neither swallow nor explain it, I "agreed" for their sakes, I thought, to go into their crummy treatment center and put in my month, and then get back to my beloved chablis.

None of that happened, of course. For in the center, I learned I was fatally ill, unable to control my drinking or manage my life, and in need of people and powers much greater than myself to restore me to sanity, to my family, to my God, and to a way of life I had loved and enjoyed for so many years.

I was lucky to have such loving but firm family members. So many families choose only to shield, to protect, to enable, and often finally to reject the drinking woman in the family.

All of us recovering alcoholic women from the "old days" are very lucky still to be around, because we had a husband or children who not only stuck with us, but finally did enough research to discover we needed treatment, AA, or both. In the past, relatively few alcoholic women received the understanding and help they needed to pursue recovery. Alcoholic women have had it tough.

HISTORICALLY TOUGH ON WOMEN

Historically, both men and women have tried to "protect" female alcoholics more systematically from stigma, but also judged them more harshly than their male counterparts, and for some obvious reasons, I think.

First and perhaps foremost: when drunken women have responsibility for the physical care of children, people judge them severely for failure to fulfill those obligations. Ironically, the value we attribute to the family has backfired, historically, upon alcoholic mothers.

Second, men have tended to shield themselves and their drinking female family members from any stigma society attached to drunken behavior. To have a drunken wife, or even a daughter, was a blow to a family's reputation in the community.

Also, in many traditional societies of the past, where male and female roles were firmly established, the alcoholic female was considered by many to be an affront to womanhood, and to all the virtues which society as a whole wanted to attribute to the human race. As a result, perhaps fewer woman drank and became alcoholic than men, but even fewer received help toward recovery.

> *Historically, both men and women have tried to "protect" female alcoholics from stigma, but also judged them more harshly . . .*

THE BIG CHANGE—IS IT REAL?

Today, however, treatment centers and recovery groups can claim large numbers of younger women, many in their teens, others working. We know them well. Many of the women involved in the creation of this chapter, in fact, entered treatment and AA within the last few years. Are they radically different from the average "oldtimer" of the past, different from an alcoholic woman like myself? Has society changed in its attitudes toward addicted women? If so, how and why?

Some changes have occurred—or better yet, seemed to have evolved—as some women in our society have evolved in their understanding of themselves, of men, and of their own role in society. As more and more women, for instance, have felt free to drink at whatever time in their life seemed appropriate, more have chosen to drink openly and in the setting they desire. More women have, therefore, come out of the closet with their drinking. Many, in fact, never try to hide their drinking from peers in their own social groupings.

Younger women often begin drinking and drugging (using pot,

pills, or cocaine) along with the boys in high school, in college, at parties, or even in the workplace. Though they usually lack the capacity for consumption of drugs their boyfriends enjoy (size limits the amounts a person can consume), they try to keep up and, unfortunately, often surpass non-alcoholic boys in abuse of alcohol and other drugs.

Also, many women now drink at bars, clubs, and parties in about the same pattern as men do, without fear of serious social repercussions. Some lonely and frustrated women even "work" the singles bars for a one night stand in about the same way their male counterparts do—a pattern of behavior unthinkable in my generation.

Significantly, however, in treatment centers and in AA most women we know believe that society continues to judge female alcoholics somewhat differently from male alcoholics. Many discover through bitter experience that their own parents or teachers, and sometimes, ministers, seemed first to shield them from stigma and then to judge them more severely than their male drinking companions.

POLYDRUG ABUSE

The plot now thickens. Because of the stigma society attaches to heavy alcohol consumption by women, more alcoholic women than men seem to mix other mood-altering drugs with alcohol.

Today we call such people "polydrug" users, chemically dependent, or cross-addicted people. Unfortunately, polydrug use is potentially more dangerous than single drug use—for instance, than drinking alcohol and alcohol alone. The reasons are simple and easy to understand.

When any person, male or female, young or old, combines drugs, especially alcohol, with other drugs such as pot, depressive or stimulant pills, or cocaine, he or she potentiates the effects of those drugs within the system. If a person drinks on top of Valium, he or she may even double the effects of both drugs.

If women or men continue to use drugs in combination, they rapidly lose control over their consumption and behavior, and descend into the nightmare of addiction much more quickly than a "pure" alcoholic might descend.

If you are a woman (or man) regularly combining alcohol with other drugs, you have good reason for seeking information about those risks through Alcoholics Anonymous, or by means of a consultation with a counselor at a treatment center.

A CHECKLIST FOR WOMEN ONLY

Check any of the following sentences that apply to you:

1. I usually drink as much or more than the men in my family or social group _Y___

2. When drinking or using other drugs, I feel the desire to be as wild and crazy as the guys _Y___

3. I like to mix other drugs, such as marijuana or tranquilizers, with alcohol _No___

4. Because of breath odor, I feel more comfortable, or less "guilty," using marijuana, pills, or cocaine, than when using alcohol _No___

5. I find myself uncomfortable around men unless I first have a drink or use some kind of drug _yes___

6. I feel that, because I am a woman, I have been unfairly criticized for drinking or using drugs; men get away with more than I do _yes___

If you check two or more of the above, you probably have developed difficulties involving the alcohol or other drugs you presently consume.

SEXUAL REACTIONS

When drunk, women sometimes make themselves vulnerable to physical and emotional abuse. Many alcoholic women (and men for that matter), wake up after a big party in bed with someone, male and sometimes female, they scarcely know, and cannot remember who did what to whom. If they have bruises or abrasions on their bodies, they cannot recall how they got them.

As a woman, you can imagine the dreadful fears you then have. Am I pregnant now or not? Have I caught a disease? From whom? Did I get beaten by my "boyfriend" for the night? What am I going to tell my parents who expected me home at midnight?

It's a nightmare well worth avoiding, and often a sign of very deep and complicated addictive illness.

For many women their problems with husbands seem to be complicated by sexual rejection. When a spouse feels unwanted by a mate, she has great difficulty creating the self-esteem necessary to fulfill the responsibilities of life.

On the most elementary level, some women experience a growing need to drink, drug, and sometimes "eat" away negative feelings. If they have children to care for, they begin then to neglect their children's most elementary needs—or worse yet, shift almost day by day from the extremes of over-protection to open hostility and rejection of them.

Housewives with children find this horrible experience almost unbearable to describe. If their husbands go to work in the morning, they may begin their secret drinking shortly afterwards, often on top of mood-altering drugs received from doctors. If the kids "bother" their mothers during these drunken moments, the mothers often lash out aggressively with tongue or, unfortunately, with hands or even blunt instruments, and then under the influence of drugs may fall asleep, often on a couch, a floor, or in a chair.

Remember, it's not only men who abuse family members. Many alcoholic women physically assault both their children and spouses. Anxiety, tension, guilt, self-hatred, and fear created by abuse of alcohol and other drugs, can lead to unthinkable forms of behavior among both men and women.

When a drinking housewife wakes up in the afternoon from the morning's bender, however, she often feels deep remorse, and resolves not only to abstain forever beginning the next day, but to make up for her failures toward family members by smothering them with attention.

As a result, many mothers, day after day, reject their children some of the time and overwhelm them with self-indulgent care the rest of the time. In the process, children may become both deeply confused and hostile. The more confused and hostile they become, the more confused, hostile and unpredictable their parents become. And to mask those awful feelings, they may drink, use drugs, and often over-eat all the more heavily.

OUR CHILDREN'S REACTIONS

Some children, especially younger ones, become so fearful over their drunken mother's safety that they refuse to leave her unattended. In effect, they become "babysitters" for their mothers. And because they fear their father's critical reaction to their mother's behavior, they may run around after her picking up lighted cigarettes falling from her fingers, or furniture she knocks down, or cleaning up the pieces of dishes she manages to break in the midst of her drunken stupors.

... many older children, believing
their mother chooses to drink and ig-
nore them, may simply reject their
mother altogether ...

By contrast, many older children, believing their mother chooses to drink and ignore them, may simply reject their mother altogether and keep out of her path of destruction as best they can. Often those older children not only refuse to bring friends home, but stop coming home themselves.

PROBLEMS WITH OUR MATE

An alcoholic woman's behavior around her husband or close boyfriend usually resembles her behavior around her children. In a single day, she might go from being lovingly indulgent toward him in the morning, cooking his breakfast and sending him off to work with a scorching kiss, to greeting him later in the day with aggressive verbal abuse—especially if he should come home unexpectedly and find her drinking.

Because the alcoholic woman usually feels repulsive, she may also suspect her husband of relationships with other women. Or, if her husband seems too religiously faithful, she suspects other women have designs upon him.

Husbands of alcoholic wives are more likely to seek divorce than wives of alcoholic husbands—perhaps because greater numbers of married men have the necessary professional and emotional skills to make a living, and find it more practical to leave their spouse than the average woman does.

Also, lots of "older" single women are quite happy to "pick off" the husband of a drunken wife, especially if he is attractive, reasonably well-off, and successful in his work. Most alcoholic women fear desertion by the men in their lives as much as anything else they may fear. Yet, they find themselves at the same time blaming their husbands for everything that goes wrong in their lives. It can be maddening and terrifying for both parties.

Though the subject is delicate, many alcoholic women, fearing rejection by husbands, also try when drunk to retaliate by pursuing their own "affairs." We have known women to "seduce" the man next door, not out of interest in him, but merely for revenge over real or imagined affairs their husbands were having. During my drinking days, I thought of doing it myself, but fortunately never got up the courage, even with bottle in hand.

When fully sober, however, most women find themselves overwhelmed with guilt, remorse, and self-hatred, and prepared to smother their husbands with pleas for acceptance and assurances that they'll quit drinking tomorrow. And because they want to believe that, both children and husband often take the alcoholic woman of the family at her word, and somehow accept her.

Ironically, like alcoholic men, women who feel deeply guilty and repentant, honestly believe they can stop drinking tomorrow. Since they have lost control over the consumption of alcohol or other drugs, however, they inevitably discover the next day they can't stop. As the book, *Alcoholics Anonymous* says, alcohol is "cunning, baffling, powerful" beyond belief for all alcoholics. The alcoholic is chronically and progressively ill, and requires special kinds of assistance for recovery from all sorts of special people.

When fully sober . . . most women find
themselves overwhelmed with guilt,
remorse, and self-hatred . . .

REPRODUCTIVE PROBLEMS

Many women find themselves peculiarly susceptible to the consumption of mood-altering chemicals before and during their period, and for simple reasons.

Most women suffer pain in varying degrees from cramps. A minority of women get through their period with merely a day or two of slight discomfort and perhaps irritability. Another minority of women endure severe menstrual symptoms which precede by as much as two weeks the actual menstrual discharge. Most women fall somewhere in between these two extremes during their menstrual periods.

Because alcoholic women, however, like all women, experience during their periods a degree of depression, irritability, restlessness, and pain, they are more likely to use alcohol or other drugs in excessive quantities during this time. Quite simply, they try to anesthetize themselves against discomfort.

As I well know, menopause is, at best, a difficult time for all women, and a critically destructive period for some women. Because of adverse emotional and physical symptoms brought on by hormonal changes taking place during the change of life, any woman susceptible to addiction to alcohol and other mood-altering drugs, runs a unique risk during this period in her life.

When people are depressed, feeling worthless and helpless, they are always tempted to use some sort of chemical to change or mask those awful feelings. Unfortunately, some women, in trying to control their feelings during menopause with alcohol and other drugs, rapidly lose control over those drugs and complicate their problems with addiction on top of other symptoms. If during menopause, a woman is also lonely and unemployed, her risks of addiction grow.

As I have learned, however, treatment centers and AA have helped many addicted women who drank either not at all or only rarely on social occasions until she reached middle age or even beyond. No matter what their age, or problems in life, women with addictive problems don't have to keep on drinking or using drugs any longer. Help is available.

REASONS FOR HOPE

Fortunately, any woman, young, older, or in between, suffering today from addictive disorders, has ample reason for hope. No matter how society may react to her problems, she now has resources for help and recovery which simply did not exist before. Many treatment centers in this country attempt to respond to the unique problems which women face in recovery, often with special programs.

In many urban areas, AA groups have as many, and often more women, than men. And whereas the traditional AA men's groups have diminished in the past decade, women's groups have sprung up all over. I belong to one myself in my hometown. Furthermore, the rapidly growing fellowship of Narcotics Anonymous currently claims as many female as male members.

For those women (and men) who suffer from compulsive eating disorders, Overeaters Anonymous has also become an invaluable group for recovery of spiritual balance, health, and well being. Many alcoholic women are also compulsive overeaters, especially of sweets. Several of the women who helped to create this chapter attend both AA and OA meetings, and benefit greatly from the combination. Since both organizations use the same Twelve Steps for recovery, it seems a "natural alliance." Women for Sobriety (WFS) also has recovery groups now in many parts of the country.

And so "the worm turns." For all we know, it may ultimately be easier in society today for most women—especially younger women—to seek help than for men.

THE ROAD TO RECOVERY

For most women (and men) the door to recovery still opens when a critically important person in their lives says, "Hey, this is enough. Stop the merry-go-round. I'm getting off. Or stop the merry-go-round, because you're getting off."

It happened to me.

Someone finally tells the alcoholic, if you don't find help and the means for recovery, you have to make it on your own in life. We won't accept your drinking any longer. Parents, or boyfriends, husbands, children, close friends, employers, or school officials say, "We cannot continue to support you, employ you, or keep you in school, if you keep on drinking and using drugs."

People close to the alcoholic practice "tough love," and give their loved ones the choice to seek help for recovery or drink and drug themselves to death, alone. By God's grace, thousands of women have, in their own ways responded to the challenge of intervention, have admitted they could not stop using alcohol or other drugs on their own, and with the help of other people found their way into AA.

ACT NOW

If you feel you have a problem with alcohol and/or other drug consumption, look into your telephone book for the Alcoholics Anonymous number, call, and ask for someone to come and visit with you.

AA will usually send a recovering woman alcoholic, who will share with you some of her experience with addiction, and give you hope and help for recovery yourself.

And regardless of how down and worthless you presently feel, you may anticipate a warm and loving reception in a good treatment center, and by fellow alcoholics and addicts in AA or NA. One of the great joys of recovery comes with the discovery of the wonderful fellowship existing everywhere throughout the country in treatment centers and in recovery groups.

Above all, we can assure you that, regardless of how you may presently be criticized by others for your drinking and drug use, such criticism need no longer deter any woman, young or older, from finding the help she needs for recovery. If you are an addicted woman, thousands of recovering women and men stand ready to welcome you with open arms into the fellowship of recovering alcoholics and addicts throughout the world.

If you feel yourself in trouble, you have nothing to lose by seeking help—except your troubles. And whatever self-esteem you may have lost in the past, you can by God's help, with the love and care of other people, and the AA program, attain a new confidence and health you may only now dream of.

Contact a woman today in your local recovery group, or call a treatment center. You alone can experience the hope which we have tried to describe.

Questions for: *Tough On Women*

1. When you lost control over your consumption of alcohol or other drugs, how did your behavior change? Give examples.

2. Why do "polydrug" users—people using more than one drug at one time—become more rapidly intoxicated and dependent upon drugs than people who abuse only alcohol?

3. If you are a mother, describe the problems your drinking or drug use created in your relationships with your children.

4. If you are married, describe the problems your drinking or drug use created in your relationship with your husband.

5. What unique advantages do you think you will enjoy as a woman during recovery from alcoholism or other forms of drug addiction?

6

Ten Tips to Avoid Slips

INTRODUCTION

In gatherings of recovering alcoholics, people speak naturally and frequently about situations which may lead to relapse back into addiction—what members of Alcoholics Anonymous and Narcotics Anonymous have for decades called "slips." By talking about potential slips, recovering addicts attempt to avoid them. By sharing the threat of relapse common to all alcoholics and addicts, recovering people in group meetings learn how to avoid that return to compulsive use of alcohol or other drugs which every AA or NA member rightly fears.

The Big Book of Alcoholics Anonymous speaks of the willingness to "go to any length" as a prerequisite for recovery from active alcoholism. Similarly, recovering people must remain willing to go to any length to avoid any and all circumstances which might lead to relapse.

In many respects, this chapter represents a compilation of common conversations which may be heard in thousands of rooms every day where AA and NA members gather to share their experiences, strength, and hope for continuing sobriety and a serene way of life—without slips.

SLIPPERY PLACES

When I first began to experience sobriety during recovery, I heard other recovering alcoholics talk about "slippery places." Through experience I rapidly learned what they meant.

In certain places and at certain times, I found myself tempted to slip or relapse into alcohol or drugs again. And as I spent time around other alcoholics, I learned that every recovering alcoholic and addict has his or her slippery places.

More accurately, every recovering addict has dangerous or tempting people, places, and things lurking in his environment, setting him up for a "slip" into the old and fatal ways of addiction.

An alcoholic friend of mine puts it this way: alcohol is "cunning, baffling, powerful," AND PATIENT! If you haven't felt the temptation to drink or use drugs yet, just wait. You will. And when it comes, you should be prepared.

THE PROBLEM OF PEOPLE

Certain people tempt us back to alcohol and drugs—often without intending to. Obviously, the people we drank with during our alcoholic "careers" tempt us even when they try not to. Whenever we gather with them socially, particularly at bars and parties, they will by free association become agents of temptations for us to slip.

Though by the grace of God I have been sober for some years, I still feel a slight desire for alcohol whenever I gather socially with my closest friend from high school and college. He and his wife are perfectly normal social drinkers. Since, however, I spent so many school years drinking with him, I still experience at least a mild urge for alcohol whenever I get together with him. In his company, a nostalgic desire for those once free and sociable drinking days emerges in my mind—without fail.

Fortunately, I don't have to stay away from him; and he doesn't feel the need to refrain from alcohol in my presence. What I do feel is the need to say to him every once in a while, "Sometimes I wish I could still drink, but I don't want to. Because I'm an alcoholic. But you go right ahead." Whenever I say that, I immediately eliminate any desire or embarrassment I feel in his presence. Also, I suspect I eliminate a slight uneasiness he feels when drinking in my presence.

Among close friends, the best way to handle my embarrassment...is to admit to alcoholism, and explain why I choose to abstain.

TIP 1.—When you get together socially with your former drinking friends, feel free to tell them you could also drink, but you won't, because you are an alcoholic. As soon as you have honestly described your feelings, you begin to gain control over them.

Among close friends, I think the best way to handle embarrassment and any temptations I might experience, is to admit to alcoholism, and explain why I choose to abstain.

Remember, however, that many of your non-alcoholic friends probably know little about alcoholism. Though they may wish you the best, they have little insight into your illness, and even less appreciation for it. You honor them by telling them what the illness of alcoholism is, and how people recover. Unless they are just plain defensive about their own consumption, they will probably appreciate hearing something from you about the nature of addiction.

TIP 2.—Among mere drinking acquaintances of the past, you must use your own judgment about admission of alcoholism. Given my social circumstances—I am regularly in public settings where alcohol is served—I find it easiest to let everyone interested know that I am alcoholic. Nothing stops a persistent host or hostess, a nagging or even pressuring acquaintance, faster than the simple words: "I'm alcoholic. I don't drink."

Even when a nice waiter or waitress asks me whether I want "a cocktail before dinner," I often say, "No thank you, I'm an alcoholic." The combination of surprise and sometimes respect appearing on the waiter's face almost justifies the procedure.

When my wife and I entertain mere acquaintances, and serve alcoholic beverages, I usually tell them I don't drink anymore. If they should ask me why, I would tell them I am alcoholic.

By the way, lots of non-alcoholic people in your world probably don't drink at all, or don't drink very much. When you were drinking or using drugs with abandon, you just didn't notice them. Since you disliked sober people, you probably never really associated with them. You will find it easier now to get along with them.

TIP 3.—If you wish to remain anonymous about your drinking, you can still say to pressuring friends and acquaintances, "I don't drink anymore. I'm allergic to alcohol. I get sick from alcohol."

In really tough spots, usually at parties, I have known young, recovering alcoholics and addicts to say to nagging acquaintances who want them to drink or drug: "Why is it so important for you that I use?"

That kind of line takes the addict off the defense and puts him on the offense—not a bad place to be when severely pressured by drinking people to slip back into the patterns of addiction.

TIP 4.—Around family members, try always to be completely open about any temptations you feel to drink or drug again. Remember, when it comes to your sobriety and health, you must put yourself "selfishly" first. If you should drink or drug again, you would become useless and even dangerous to those you live with. Let them know what you must do to stay clean and sober.

When family members drink or drug, and make you nervous, especially during the first months of your recovery, talk things over with them honestly and openly, and ask them not to drink or drug. If they don't refrain in your presence, say to them, "My sobriety may depend upon your cooperation." If they still don't refrain from using in your presence, you may have to take other steps to prevent yourself from falling into temptations created by those persons closest to you in your own home.

I have known a few alcoholics who have separated or even divorced over this issue. Alcoholism is not child's play. When the Big Book of AA says we must be ready to go any lengths necessary for sobriety, it means just that.

Most loving family members, however, will refrain from drinking in our presence, without our asking. Most members of our family will happily help us remove alcohol, or other drugs, from our homes to ease us toward a happy sobriety. Other alcoholics, however, find even at the beginning of their recovery that drinking family members or close friends seem to provide no threat to their own sobriety. If such is the case with you, take the time to let your friends and family know that they may continue, if they wish, to drink in patterns normal to them. Ironically, many non-alcoholic persons assume, without even thinking, that their drinking will "tempt" you back into the habit. You may have to "free them up" to continue their own patterns of moderate consumption.

TIP 5.—If parents and other relatives are extremely negative about drinking and drunkenness, or seem unable to accept the reality of your alcoholism, do not push the issue upon them. If you have to push, you will at that very moment feel guilty over your own illness around your relatives. And that sort of guilt often translates into the urge to drink.

Because of personal sensitivities, some parents cannot accept addiction in their children. If your parents are so threatened, you really have no right and certainly no reason to force them into acceptance. When your family members feel forced to deny the reality of the problem you cannot expect them to accept alcoholism any more easily than you did. Give your parents or other relatives permission not to talk about alcoholism. I have many relatives who never speak about the subject in my presence. I assume they have their reasons. Either they find it too embarrassing for themselves, or they wish to protect my feelings. In either case, their decision belongs to them.

TIP 6.—If your home is itself a place of temptation for you, you must do everything possible within the home to reduce the possibility of slips.

I was a home drinker. Early in my recovering days, therefore, I thought it best to keep all alcohol and all mood-altering medications out of my house.

Since I worried a lot about insomnia, I found the middle of the night a particularly tempting time. When I can't sleep, I still sometimes think to myself, "A belt of this, or a capsule of that, would certainly solve my problems for the night."

However, if I have nothing on hand, I'm not likely to trot off in the middle of the night to some store for booze. I haven't done it yet. Usually, I've gone to sleep on my own, and forgot about the urge altogether.

TIP 7.—Stay out of all places which induce in you anything even resembling an urge to drink. A mere thought, of course is not an urge.

I have lunch regularly with an old AA friend in a restaurant with a bar. Frequently, the sight of men and women hoisting down cold ones at the rail reminds me of my past drinking days. I may think of having a drink, but feel no urge to do so. If ever I felt a real urge, or above all a compulsion, for a beer or martini, I would beat a retreat and not come back.

Don't take chances. If you drank or used drugs for years with a particular group of people hanging out in a particular bar, I think you should avoid that place and find new friends, perhaps in AA or in Narcotics Anonymous.

In my association with alcoholics, both as a friend and sometimes a counselor, I have found that many persons are unable to return to old drinking and drugging haunts and remain free from the temptation to use again. We addicts remember our old drugged and drunken feelings. We remember which door led to the pot, and where the coke was snorted. And when everyone else in our crowd persists in using, we find ourselves sometimes driven to participate—or to feeling sorry for ourselves because we can't participate.

When gathering with the old drinking crowd, younger alcoholics in particular often feel they can't act "crazy, wild, and free" without the benefit of a drug. The urge to create the old and carefree person of the past may become overwhelming. When that need arises, we should beat a fast retreat to our new crowd in AA or Narcotics Anonymous.

By avoiding both the people and the places of addiction, we also avoid the need to save people from their problems. Whatever else we recovering alcoholics might be into, we're not into the salvation or the therapy business. Our own sobriety is challenge enough. Unless we are professionally trained and prepared, we dare not set out to heal the world. When a real friend reveals a need for help, we shall find the way to provide it. We think it's best, however, for our sobriety, not to push sobriety on people who seem to have no present desire for it.

TIP 8.—A rule of thumb: when you sense a place might be tempting, IT WILL BE TEMPTING. If it seems tempting already in your mind, it will probably be tempting in reality.

I have an alcoholic salesman acquaintance who, after years of sobriety, still refuses to drive past old drinking places in the cities and towns he visits on his routes. I admire his caution.

Many alcoholics decide never again to stop near a liquor store, or even a particular grocery store where they once bought their alcohol. I have known alcoholics never to play golf again because they sense they might not be able to resist a quick cold one in the 19th Hole Bar.

Tempting places may include your favorite vacation haunts, which in reality were your favorite watering holes. Drinking alcoholics choose vacation spots largely for their drinking possibilities. Everyone drinks at the beach or on a cruise, right? That may be reason enough for you to avoid the beach or that cruise. Everyone drinks on holidays, at Fourth of July picnics, and New Year's Eve parties. That may be reason enough for you to avoid certain parties.

If in doubt about a place or situation, avoid it, and go to an AA meeting instead.

TIP 9.—Avoid those physical and emotional situations which tempt you to drink and use again. Recovering people like to remind themselves of slippery states of mind by using the acronym, HALT. HALT stands for "hungry, angry, lonely, tired." Hunger, anger, loneliness, and fatigue are feelings and conditions to avoid at all costs in order to maintain a good sobriety.

Maybe, you're already saying to yourself, how "simplistic" and corny. Obviously, everyone, alcoholic or not, should try to avoid hunger, anger, loneliness and fatigue, you say. You are right. Since most of us alcoholics, however, are compulsive by nature, we have a lot of trouble doing obviously necessary things to avoid further trouble with alcohol and drugs.

When sober many of us tend to work too hard too long, often to make up for time lost during our drinking days. Many of us play too hard and too long, sometimes following old patterns of self-indulgence, but now without alcohol. We may eat too little or too much of the wrong foods at the wrong times. Often we don't get enough sleep, or keep such outrageous hours that we fail to obtain necessary rest.

Destructive anger may be the toughest of all emotions for alcoholics to avoid. During our drinking days, we got into the habit of angrily blaming other people and things for our problems and flying into a state of outrage at the slightest provocation. We have great trouble in sobriety ridding ourselves of habitual patterns of self-pitying and resentful thinking. As you feel anger toward other people or events build up within, try as best you can to turn that anger over to God as you understand Him, and get it out of your system. Try, especially, to avoid self-pitying and resentful thoughts in the evenings before you go to sleep.

Many an alcoholic has in the dead of the night slipped back to alcohol or pills simply because he or she has fallen into a deadly cycle of resentful thoughts, which build and build to the thought: "In this state of mind I really deserve a drink. Or a pill to put me to sleep." And feeling quite justified, the alcoholic decides to take something for the night, only to discover the next day he can't stop drinking or drugging in the old patterns of addiction.

A recovering alcoholic friend of mine says, "I come close to a slip whenever I have 'stacked problems.'" I love the phrase. By it, he means one thing after another, family, job, or health problems, stacking up one upon the other until they seem about to break him.

When that happens to us, it's time to HALT, take stock, set our priorities in line, and get to them. Many of us have slipped back into addiction because we simply failed to tackle the problems of life, one by one, one day at a time, with a sense of discipline. Unconsciously, we began to think: a little drink will surely help us past the hump. Or fearing breakdown, we drank and really broke down—down the drain. And coming back to sobriety and second or third time can be so much harder that the first.

TIP 10.—Our final tip for you is to try your best when sober to maintain your normal capacities to fulfill basic needs in life.

When I find myself undermining my basic human needs, it is time to set my priorities very carefully. When I discover myself too tired and nervous to function sexually, too anxious to sleep, and too gassy or peptic to eat and digest food with my normal regularity, I know I have failed to follow my own daily schedule of exercise, eating, and sleeping.

Since alcoholism is a physical, emotional, and spiritual illness, I try to do something physically, emotionally, and spiritually uplifting everyday of my recovery.

MY PROGRAM FOR RECOVERY

For the sake of emotional stability, I try especially during difficult periods of my life to go to AA meetings at least every other day. If I need help in sorting out my priorities, I ask for it from my AA sponsor, my wife, and from good friends.

For sake of physical health, I try to eat three relatively fat-free meals each day, exercise either at tennis or racquetball with friends or on my bike at least 20 minutes every other day. I try to go to bed by 10:30 P.M. to get a minimum of eight hours of sleep or rest. I also refuse caffeine after my noon meal, eat only a light snack before bed, and do not smoke. Though coffee has long been a mainstay beverage in the AA fellowship, many of us consume enough caffeine, day and night, to threaten both our emotional and physical health. And need we mention that too many alcoholics consume altogether too much of that common, legal, but destructive, drug nicotine?

For the sake of spiritual health, I read, pray, and meditate each morning and evening. I would urge you to establish your own pattern of spiritual exercise and growth, and try to stick to it.

As I try to keep my "schedule" day by day, I discover that I largely eliminate angry and resentful feelings from my life. Since most of the anger we feel toward others is anger we feel primarily for ourselves, we cut down on our capacity for resentment toward others as we try to live up to our own expectations.

Though I know my daily patterns will fit only my life and not necessarily yours, a regular pattern of living which keeps hunger, anger, loneliness, and fatigue at a minimum is strongly recommended for all recovering alcoholics.

THE POWER OF CHOICE

Whenever you are in a slippery place, remember: as a sober person you have freedom and power of choice. When drunk you give up your freedom of choice, and place yourself under the power of a drug. So, whatever happens in a slippery place, choose sobriety above all, and you will probably not slip—with or without these tips.

Take them, however, and make of them what you need and wish for your life, and for those whom you love in your world.

Questions for: *Ten Tips To Avoid Slips*

1. Give one example of how you can use each tip described in this booklet as an aid to your sobriety.

2. AA members often talk about "people, places, and things," which tempt them to return to active alcoholism or drug addiction. Write down a half dozen people, places, or things which you think would tempt you to slip.

3. If you plan to return to a drinking social group or society, how do you plan to explain your own abstinence? What will you tell your relatives? Your closest friends? Your acquaintances, or new people you meet?

4. If you have close family members who cannot accept the reality of your alcoholism or addiction, how do you plan to handle this situation?

5. Recovering alcoholics try to avoid getting too hungry, angry, lonely or tired. Why are those conditions and feelings dangerous for the alcoholic or addict?

7

Victory During Vulnerable Times

INTRODUCTION

All alcoholics and addicts are liable to lapse or "slip" into previous patterns of alcohol and drug consumption. Alcoholics Anonymous rightfully calls its members "recovering" alcoholics or addicts. Statistics indicate that very few, if any, abstinent alcoholics or addicts can ever return to the chemicals they abused in the past, without becoming compulsively addicted to them again.

For that reason, times of crisis in a recovering alcoholic's or addict's life become critically vulnerable times. As an alcoholic responds to severe loss, failure, bad health, or the threat of terminal illness, he or she is naturally inclined to return to those mood-altering drugs which offered short-term relief from depression and anxiety in the past. Unfortunately, the addicted person who follows this inclination will in all likelihood discover himself or herself trapped again by an ever-growing compulsion to use and abuse the very drugs which once provided temporary relief.

The following chapter was written by a person who had first-hand experience with a life crisis, and relapsed. It provides ways and means for addicted people to avoid relapse during vulnerable times. Above all, the chapter offers hope, even to those recovering people who discover that they have problems which may prove terminal.

Without hope, no addicted person in good times or bad will experience continuing recovery from addiction. This chapter is dedicated to the possibility of hope, even and especially for the most desperate of people.

MY EXPERIENCE

As a recovering alcoholic vulnerable to major losses in life, I can best begin this chapter by describing my one great slip in 15 years of sobriety. I have learned more about potential relapse during that one terrible experience than from all the words I have heard from others.

It happened this way. After I had been sober for about eight years, my father died suddenly of stroke-related illnesses. Though I had for some time anticipated it, his death hit me with the force of a truck. In a considerable daze, I traveled about 400 miles to my parents' home to gather with my family members and to attend my father's funeral.

Surrounded by family members at the funeral, however, I felt reasonably strong, secure, and calm. Though I felt deeply moved by grief during the service, I did not come close to losing my emotional balance. I came home afterward believing that I had managed the loss well. Above all, I believed I had successfully resisted a relapse into alcoholic drinking during a uniquely stressful time in my life.

COMING HOME

When I got home and back to work, however, the bottom simply dropped out of my emotions. On the very first morning I experienced overwhelming grief and confusion. And though I tried to restrain myself, I woke up day after day thereafter, literally crying. In a short time, I slipped into a moderate depression.

As my mind circled back to my early years with my father, I first recalled over and over again what seemed to me the many ways in which I had failed my father, and then the many ways in which he had seemed to fail me. And though I tried to stop thinking in this pattern, I could not overcome the massive feelings of anger and guilt that had suddenly overwhelmed me. And because my father had died I could neither share my feelings with him nor ask for forgiveness. I felt trapped.

Though I know now I should have talked about my emotions with my AA sponsor, or a pastor, and gone to my regular AA meetings, I kept my emotions bottled up within myself. Having grown up in a restrained family, it was difficult for me to speak of my shock or grief even to family members. That was almost a fatal mistake. Unconsciously, I was setting the stage for a return to alcohol.

About a week after the funeral I awoke from a restless sleep, and felt an immediate and powerful compulsion for alcohol. To this day I cannot fully describe the sensation. I had never had it before, and thank God, have not had it since. All I can say is this: my body and mind seemed suddenly to cry out for a drink. I could almost taste it in the back of my throat!

Telling my wife I wanted to get a newspaper, I left the house, bought a bottle of chablis and downed it in what seemed about sixty seconds in a parking lot. I came home drunk—and without a paper. In the following weeks, I kept drinking on a daily basis and rapidly lost control of my consumption and my behavior. After years of sobriety, I was on my way back into treatment for alcoholism.

> *. . . when we alcoholics experience unusually strong emotions . . . we are often tempted . . . to excessive consumption.*

WHY DID I SLIP?

Could I have prevented the slip? To answer that question we have first to determine why alcoholics so often fall back upon mood-altering chemicals for relief during times of severe loss and pain.

When human beings lose a loved one, their health, a job, or a spouse through divorce, they experience unique reactions of shock, grief, confusion, anger, depression, and often guilt. During such a period, most people feel strange and disoriented, and some experience a temporary need for alcohol or other drugs to relieve discomforting symptoms. Even good feelings—highs—throw people off stride and make them for at least a brief moment feel as if they are not "really" themselves.

When San Diego first baseman, Steve Garvey, hit a home run in the ninth inning of the fourth game of the 1984 playoff series against Chicago, he said: "As I watched the ball sail toward the fence, time seemed for a brief moment to stop. When it went over the fence, everything started up again." Garvey had a normal reaction to a supremely "high" experience.

Unfortunately, when we alcoholics experience unusually strong emotions, good or painful, we are often tempted, because of a learned pattern of reaction in the past, to reduce or increase our feelings through excessive consumption of mood-altering chemicals. If we are overpowered by such experiences, we may feel a need literally to anesthetize ourselves by getting drunk or stoned, even though we may plan to have only a few drinks, a joint, or a few pills for temporary relief. As recovering alcoholics frequently say of alcohol: we used it to "solve" our problems in the past; we know we can always use it again. An alcoholic's memory is longer than an elephant's.

In retrospect, I believe I began thinking of a drink immediately after receiving the news of my father's death. I even dreamed one night after the funeral that I had taken a drink at a party and had been caught by my wife—a common type of dream among alcoholics fearful of a slip. Though I blocked the thought out of my conscious thinking during the funeral, I allowed it to surface in my unconscious thinking after I got back. And very gradually, the thought entered my conscious thinking as well.

Though my father had been ill for years, I had not worked through my feelings toward him, and had failed to prepare myself for the impact of his death. When the loss came, therefore, I seemed unable to apply my recovery program to this utterly new set of experiences.

Somehow I convinced myself I could use alcohol for temporary relief only—a potentially fatal conclusion for alcoholics.

Deep down inside, I came to believe slowly but surely that I could handle my grief, anger, and guilt feelings best by resorting temporarily to alcohol as an anesthetic. Somehow I convinced myself I could use alcohol for *temporary* relief only—a potentially fatal conclusion for alcoholics. It is amazing and frightening for me to realize just how quickly and powerfully such deceptive thinking can surface under stress, even after years of good sobriety.

VULNERABLE TIMES

If you are a recovering person and face any one or more of the following situations in your life, you will probably experience some need and temptation to return for relief to drugs you previously abused. If you presently have the feelings described in these statements, you should speak as soon as possible to your AA or NA sponsor, your AA or NA group, to a doctor or counselor at a treatment center, or to someone, a minister perhaps, familiar with the disease of addiction.

1. I have recently lost a parent and feel deeply grieved and even guilty over his or her death.

2. I have lost a spouse, or a child, and find myself numbed, lonely, and in a state of shock.

3. My parents have recently decided to get a divorce, and I feel angry, depressed, and simply unable to accept their decision.

4. One of my children has gotten himself or herself into deep trouble with alcohol, drugs, promiscuity, or the police, and I feel both terribly angry and guilty over his or her behavior.

5. My spouse has recently made the decision to divorce me, and I feel shocked, angry, and unsure of how I am going to survive by myself.

6. I have just been fired or suspended from my job, and feel angry, guilty, and worthless.

7. One of the members of my household has a terminal illness, physical or emotional, and I feel sorrow, embarrassment, and resentment about the whole situation.

8. I have received a diagnosis of severe or possibly terminal illness, and find myself denying the diagnosis, angry at God or fate, bargaining with God for healing, constantly depressed, or all of the above.

In the last instance, you must at all costs talk, even if talk seems impossible, immediately to your sponsor, to a counselor or doctor at a treatment center, and, if you have one, to your minister, priest or rabbi.

WHY AREN'T WE PREPARED?

Many of us, I think, fail to make emotional and spiritual prepa-
rations for losses in life, and for two reasons. One, we don't want to
think about disasters in life, and like to feel that we are immune to
them. And two, we have difficulty, in our secular culture, thinking and
talking about potential losses in meaningful, spiritual terms. Though
we know intellectually about the possibilities of illness, temporary and
terminal, of injury, or death, most of us feel on average days to be
"above" such catastrophes. As people frequently say in the face of a
severe loss, "I always thought such things happened only to other
people." One of my closest friends likes to say, laughingly, "I'll start
worrying about death when I'm sixty-five."

By blocking our minds against disaster, however, we may also
render ourselves severely vulnerable to shock when disaster strikes.
Without a relationship with helping people and some kind of Power
greater than ourselves in life, we may find ourselves suddenly unable
to manage by ourselves.

I have seen it happen to dozens of alcoholic people. Something like
that happened to me at the time of my father's death.

Through the AA program, I had prepared myself against a slip
resulting from too much complacency. I had tried to "HALT" whenever
I felt myself becoming overly hungry, angry, lonely, or tired, and tried
to take the necessary steps to remedy these problems. Through attendance at AA meetings and weekly conversations with my sponsor, I
had tried to free myself from resentments and frustration, especially
over fellow human beings. I had kept up a fairly regular daily discipline
of prayer and meditation. In the face of death, however, I still had no
resources upon which I could draw to handle my unresolved feelings
about my father.

For the alcoholic, the unexpectedly intense emotion is one key to
the possibility of relapse. What we have previously experienced and
weathered, we believe we can weather again. What we have never
experienced, we may find unbearable, and then decide by default that
we can cope with our feelings only through the means we employed in
the past—with alcohol or a similar mood-altering drug. What alter-
natives do we have? Where and how can we learn about the dangers
we face during vulnerable times in our lives?

For the alcoholic, the unexpectedly intense emotion is one key to the possibility of relapse.

SPEAKING OF LOSS

To handle loss healthily, I have discovered that I must find a setting in which I can talk about the possibilities of loss. I benefit especially from successful veterans of severe losses, who can share the feelings they have experienced. As I listen to them, I discover how I might also respond to loss without resorting to mood-altering chemicals. I encourage you to do the same.

If we can't find a family member from whom we may learn, we can with effort find a supporting person, perhaps in AA, or in a church fellowship, or on a treatment center staff, to help us learn how to cope with losses in our lives, no matter what happens in the future. Most importantly, we should try to find someone who has already experienced crises in life and turned them over to others, and to a God of their understanding. He or she can become for us an invaluable source of support, guidance, and potential relief when such sufferings come.

My AA sponsor is a diabetic with a history of heart attacks and congestive heart failure. He has lost a leg to diabetes, has lost a teenage son, has gone through a divorce, and has obviously faced up to the reality of terminal illness and death. With the help of the AA program, however, he has been able to turn his life over successfully to God as he understands Him, and lives a life of considerable serenity. Because of my relationship with him, I know that I can talk to him about potential problems and crises in my own life, and also turn to him for help should I experience severe losses which I cannot handle.

In conversations with him, I can also learn how to avoid critical mistakes in my marriage or in my work. Since he is my sharpest critic, he is quite willing to let me know when I am flirting with disaster—especially during those periods when I am working too hard, or on the verge of "burning out." Many of us alcoholics need someone close to us who will say, "Your motor is running too fast," or "You're worrying too much about your ego and too little about your sobriety. Set your priorities and stay sober!"

In this way my sponsor helps me both to prevent unnecessary losses, and to confront inevitable problems (and even my own death) as best I can when they come.

WHEN DISASTER STRIKES

What can we do to handle our feelings soberly when disaster does occur in our lives?

1. We should try to "let out" our emotions at the time the loss occurs. None of us really has anything to gain by holding back our true feelings of grief or anger in the face of unexpected catastrophes. If I had been able at the time of my father's death simply to share my feelings even with my wife, I believe I would not have allowed myself to be driven later on to anesthetize them with alcohol. When we experience real grief, we need people with whom we can express it. As we share it, we also air it, and reduce the tensions we experience.

2. We should try to talk as rationally as we can about bad experiences within close relationships we already enjoy—particularly among family members and close friends. If we worry about how we look during periods of grief, we can still call people on the phone. Most of our friends will be honored that we allow them to share our burden during times of real stress.

Some years ago, a close friend from the midwest called me on a Saturday morning from his office. With a broken voice, he managed to tell me he was feeling a little faint and just felt the need to talk. When I asked him why, he said that his son had been killed in an auto accident during the week, and had been buried just the day before.

Because I felt honored by his trust in me, I eagerly spoke to him about his loss, and shared some of my own similar experiences. By the time we finished the conversation, I believe he had recovered some of his emotional balance. And I had found another place I could turn when I next experienced losses in my own life.

3. We need to get out of our houses and into the fresh air—especially if we feel an urge or compulsion to drink. Though most of us in times of great grief do not want to shop, or entertain ourselves or others, we can at least move about each day and change our setting. Even a short walk can often

clear the head, and relieve us from preoccupation. I have found that the mere sights and sounds of nature can help me toward recovery from grief.

4. We should learn as quickly as possible to get back to a normal pattern of work and play, and build confidence in our ability to continue in life despite our loss. As we get back into our regular patterns of life, we discover that other people will respect our feelings, and will admire us for bearing up under them. Though they may not be wrapped up in our problems, they will usually be sympathetic to our needs, and help us bear our burdens.

5. If we believe in a God, and have a regular pattern of spiritual exercise, we should by all means continue in whatever discipline we follow: prayer, devotion, meditation, and gathering with other people for worship and communion with God, even if we feel at that time that we do not fully "believe" in God. Depression tends to eliminate feelings of faith. Yet it is exactly during those periods of stress that we need God and supportive people above everything else.

. . . when resentments loom large, so also does the temptation to escape . . . into alcohol.

Based upon my experience, I do not believe I could ever talk or "pray" myself out of stressful feelings during difficult periods in life. I believe God and other people, however, can lift me out in spite of myself. At least during those times of loss and failure, I do not feel as if I can manage my life by myself. In times of grief, we must try our best to turn our losses over to a Power greater than ourselves. When we can place them into the hands of God, we find the burdens we carry greatly lightened.

JOB LOSS

From my own and other's experience, I have discovered that the loss of a job creates emotions similar to those we undergo during the loss of a loved one—with some differences. When we lose a job, we are much more likely to experience rage and guilt, and for good reasons.

When we lose a job, we usually experience feelings of personal failure affecting both our own self-esteem, and the esteem others give us. If we feel we have been unfairly treated by our employer, we may find ourselves also awash in resentments we simply cannot handle. And when resentments loom large, so does the temptation to escape—justifiably we may think—into alcohol.

As Bill Wilson, co-founder of AA, once wrote, "(For an alcoholic) resentment is the number one offender."

When we experience failures in life, we must do our best to turn our failures over into God's hands, and let Him take them from us. Though it is difficult to do, we must also try to talk as frankly and honestly as possible with family members and friends about the reality of our failures. When we talk about failure, we begin to forgive ourselves and in the process discover that others still accept us, and usually find those failures to be far less serious than we think. When we begin to accept our failures in the same way, we can also begin to rectify them.

If we feel personally responsible for a job loss, we must be especially quick to share our failures with others. Failures shared are failures shed, while hidden failures fester.

When we lose a job, we may discover that we are not one of a kind. In the AA fellowship, for instance, we may meet many people, young and older, who have lost jobs for all sorts of reasons, often due to alcoholic behavior. When sober AA members, however, accept responsibilities for their job losses, confront them, share them, try to make amends and move on courageously to the next opportunities, they usually find new employment and new rewards.

Self-pity and resentment won't help us find another job. AA members calls these feelings, "stinking thinking." But courage and honesty can enable us to start looking for a new job. A new job may, in fact, be better than the old one. God does often move in mysterious ways in our own lives.

When we talk about failure, we dis-
cover that others still accept us,
and . . . find those failures . . . far less
serious than we think.

DIVORCE AND OTHER LOSSES

Divorced people have feelings very similar to those experienced by those who lose a loved one. Even when a divorced person feels there were good grounds for divorce, he will usually find himself angry, and feeling guilty, depressed, and lonely when the divorce is completed.

Because a divorced person feels like a failure in life, he or she must try to air and share those feelings with others who have had similar experience with divorce. Since many AA and Al-Anon members have gone through a divorce, these fellowships provide healthy opportunities for mutual sharing of the divorce experience.

Because therapists say it takes an average divorced person a minimum of two years to adjust to a new single way of life, the divorcee must be patient and courageous in the early days and months after a divorce becomes final. Divorced persons, for instance, may also literally find themselves out of touch with current codes of conduct applying to dating, "courtship," living together or pursuing a marriage. Too often, a divorced person jumps from the frying pan into the fire by rushing into a new marriage.

No matter what the failure we experience, we must be prepared to accept realistically our own contributions to that failure. Unless we face our own behavior honestly, we usually resort to self-pity and resentment in order to excuse our experiences to ourselves and others. And no matter what the cause, such feelings always create a fertile soil in which the compulsion for alcohol or similar drugs may easily grow.

DEATH SENTENCE

Even if I should develop a life threatening or crippling illness— heart attack, stroke, cancer—I have learned again from dozens of recovering people both in AA and Al-Anon, that I do not have to give up hope and turn to alcohol and drugs for relief—unless I choose to.

I have met dozens of people, in addition to my own sponsor, in AA and Al-Anon, in church groups, and among treatment center staff, who have accepted a diagnosis of crippling or terminal illness, have shared their feelings with both healthy and sick persons close to them, and have turned their anxiety, depression, anger, and self-pity, into the hands of a God whom they came to believe was stronger even than death.

My terminally ill friends in AA down through the years have consistently told me: in AA or Al-Anon, you can always find people facing the same problems you face. When your time comes, they tell me, find those people, share with them, learn from them, and so carry the load together.

If you presently suffer from a crippling or terminal illness, and don't believe what I'm saying, ask within your AA fellowship, or your church, at your treatment center, for people who can help you. The people are out there for you, and with effort you can find them.

WHEN COMPULSION STRIKES

When we do feel an urge, or especially a compulsion, to drink or drug, we must immediately do everything possible to counteract those feelings. Compulsions are deadly temptations, and cannot be taken lightly.

Based upon the experiences of many alcoholics who have slipped, I would encourage the following procedures. When feeling a compulsion to drink or use drugs, sit down and think as clearly as possible about the consequences.

Do you really want to slip back into the nightmare of alcoholic drinking? Do you really believe you can take just a few drinks, a joint, or pills? Think of your last drinking episode and the price you paid for it. Read your favorite sections from the Big Book of Alcoholics Anonymous, especially those sections which warn against slips.

Call your sponsor—before you drink, not after. Keep telephone numbers of AA members in your possession (I have a dozen or so in my wallet) so that you can reach someone—perhaps more than one—and talk. Share the exact feelings you experience. Be honest. Your fellow alcoholics will identify with your feelings, and help you conquer the urge to consume mood-altering chemicals.

When feeling a compulsion to drink, we alcoholics enter a panic state. For a brief time, we feel as if we can't survive without alcohol, a pill, a joint, or a line of cocaine. If we can get past those overwhelming feelings of panic, however, we shall regain a measure of equilibrium. The trick is to get past the crisis point without drinking.

If the feeling of panic seems to persist, try to get to AA meetings at least once a day. I have known alcoholics under stress to go to meetings morning, noon, and night. Repeat the Serenity Prayer as often as you can. Live hour by hour, or moment by moment, and turn every moment and every hour into the hands of God, as you understand Him.

If the panic becomes truly overwhelming, contact your local alcoholism treatment center and ask to speak to a counselor on staff. With the help of God and other people, you can face your desire for alcohol and drugs without a slip even during the most vulnerable times.

For now, try to be honest about your deepest and most powerful feelings in life. Reflect upon them and share them with others. What you can bring to the surface now in peaceful times will threaten you far less in vulnerable times. Be prepared by sharing your life, as best you can, with the people closest to you in your family, and in AA or Al-Anon.

AFTER A SLIP

If you slip back into alcohol or other drugs, you will inevitably feel defeated, depressed, guilty, and hopeless. Unless you keep on drinking, however, you have no real reason to lose hope. What can you do after a slip?

With the help of God and other people, you can face your desire for alcohol and drugs without a slip . . .

Share your slip with your sponsor and other close friends in your AA home group. Don't hide it! The longer you keep it to yourself, the more likely you will keep drinking.

If you don't have a sponsor or home group, you can share your slip with people you already know in AA. They won't be shocked, I assure you. And you will be pleasantly surprised at the relief you feel when you get the slip off your chest.

When I shared my relapse some years ago with my home group, I was vastly relieved and overjoyed to discover that my fellow AA members not only accepted me, but admired me for my honesty. After I began to share my experiences, I discovered that other alcoholics and similar addicts have relapses back into alcoholic behavior, but do recover again when they continue to pursue a program of recovery.

If we continue to slip day by day back into alcohol or other drugs, hopefully our family members and friends will confront us with the danger we face, and induce us back into inpatient or outpatient therapy at a treatment center. In relapse, most of us alcoholics deteriorate rapidly. Unless we make every effort to halt our drinking again, we shall inevitably move quickly toward insanity or drug-related death. After relapse, alcoholic drinking becomes particularly threatening— a duel with death itself.

Remember: there is no problem in your life which a drink will not make worse!

VICTORY

Most importantly for anyone facing vulnerable times in life: thousands of recovering alcoholics and similar addicts have proven their ability to remain sober during the toughest times imaginable: a death in the family, the loss of a job, or of a marriage, or even a diagnosis of terminal illness. Their success stories give us hope that we can do the same. If we want to stay sober, and are willing to take the proper steps, we can cope soberly with any crisis in our lives.

Remember: there is no problem in your life which a drink will not make worse!

We invite you to turn your losses and failures into the hands of God, as you understand Him, and into the hands of people whom you like and love. With the help of others, you can continue even in the midst of great adversity, to live a sober and serene life. Thousands of recovering alcoholics provide living proof of that promise.

Questions for: *Victory During Vulnerable Times*—

1. What does it feel like to relapse into drinking or drug use after a period of abstinence? How did those feelings tip you off that you were on your way toward a "slip"—a relapse?

2. Recovering alcoholics under stress often repeat the acronymn, HALT, to prepare against relapse into drinking or drug use. What do the letters stand for? How might you use the letters during vulnerable times?

3. A person who experiences severe loss or failure recovers more quickly without using alcohol or drugs for relief when he or she shares his or her feelings with others. Why do you think that is true?

4. If you should lose a job, what are the first things you would do to get through the experience without resorting to alcohol or other drugs?

5. A sponsor is a close acquaintance from AA who provides counsel and other help to a recovering alcoholic. Do you think a sponsor would be helpful for your recovery? Explain. How do you plan to get a sponsor?

6. If you should have a slip or relapse into the use of alcohol or similar drugs, describe a plan for action for yourself to overcome the relapse.

8

Living With the Blues

INTRODUCTION

The blues strike alcoholics and non-alcoholics alike. Researchers say that probably 25 percent of all Americans experience depressed feelings at any given time. Though some people claim they have never had such feelings, the vast majority of people experience depression at various times in their lives, some many times, and a small percentage most of the time.

Doctors divide depressed persons into two basic types, and thereafter into various sub-types. People who get depressed at bad situations and events they call exogenous depressives. Those who regularly get depressed inside, without particular outside stimulus, they call endogenous.

Since we find that the symptoms of depression are the same, we write this chapter for both "inside" and "outside" depressives. Those of us who get depressed on a regular or chronic basis may have more difficulties in life than those who feel blue on an irregular or reactive basis. From experience, however, we have discovered that we can do many things to cope with our feelings—no matter what sort of depressed person we might be.

Doing something about depressed feelings is especially vital for alcoholics and similar addicts like ourselves. Unfortunately, many chemically dependent people use symptoms of depression as a convenient "excuse" to use mood-altering drugs, especially alcohol, tranquilizers, and more recently cocaine. When a dependent person uses drugs to alleviate anxiety or depression, he may not only increase the symptoms he wants to relieve, but will rapidly lose control over the consumption of the alcohol or other drugs he thinks will help him.

WHAT IS DEPRESSION?

Since many depressed people don't know they're depressed, or don't want to admit so, we begin by describing depression.

If outside events make us feel blue, we will usually experience a certain amount of self-pity. Some people call this experience the PLOM syndrome—the "poor, little, ol' me" pattern of thinking. The PLOM pattern is a common and recurring state of mind for many people. Most people work their way through these feelings and get over them. Some, however, may not be aware of the self-pity they experience, and imagine that it stems from "justified resentment" toward someone or something which has caused them harm. If they continue to harbor self-pity over a period of time, however, it will turn into full-scale resentment, difficult to overcome. Both self-pity and resentment are symptoms of developing depression.

Since resentful alcoholics so often become drinking alcoholics, self-pity becomes for them a potentially deadly feeling. The Big Book of Alcoholics Anonymous calls resentment the "number one offender."* When resentful, an alcoholic not only feels the need to rid himself or herself of discomfort through alcohol, but also feels justified in doing so.

"If so-and-so thinks he can do this to me and get away with it, I'll show him. I'll get drunk. So there!" the alcoholic says to himself. And thus he goes down the drain of compulsive drinking once again, and inevitably becomes even more seriously depressed.

Though we cannot prevent feelings of self-pity from arising within us, we can respond to them effectively and get rid of them. If we are on our guard we can also keep self-pity from turning into destructive resentment.

If we cannot respond effectively to threatening outside events, we shall, unfortunately, begin to feel at first helpless, then relatively hopeless, and finally worthless. Unless we fall back upon chemicals to cope with depressing events, however, we don't have to allow even these feelings to become chronic. We can find the ways to change them. We shall try to describe them later in this chapter.

*From Chapter 5 of *Alcoholics Anonymous*. Reprinted by permission.

ANXIOUS PEOPLE

As contradictory as it seems, anxious people are usually depressed; depressed people are usually anxious—some more so than others. Doctors like to talk about anxiety-prone people and depression-prone people. Actually, these may be the same people, prone to feelings of helplessness, but reacting in slightly different ways because of different experiences.

As a rule of thumb, we tend to become depressed when we feel guilty or resentful over the past. We tend to become anxious when we feel fearful of someone or something, and when we face challenges and changes in the future. Guilt feelings and failures carried over from the past aggravate and increase anxiety feelings, which is one reason why depression and anxiety frequently come and go together.

Highly anxious people have trouble sleeping, perspire in normal temperatures, pace, elevate their heart rate, may have facial tics, shakes, have their "minds elsewhere," and may experience panic attacks in fearful and stressful situations. These situations may include the speaker's podium, crowded rooms, high places, enclosed places, and the local supermarket.

When anxious, in fact, we may become frightened about almost anything. For years, I panicked over the possibility of not going to sleep, and forgetting the words for the many speeches and lectures I must give in my line of work. That was my peculiar panic button. As a doctor friend of mine likes to say, "Your ticket was punched that way. Because of something that happened to you in your youth, you worry a lot about sleep as a preparation for competition with your peers."

Though I don't worry as much, I still panic from time to time over the possibility of insomnia the night before I must make a speech. It sounds silly, unless it has happened to you.

No anxiety attacks are silly, I assure you. Yours are no sillier than mine. Most anxious people struggle heroically beyond the imagination of healthier people to control their anxieties. Because anxiety symptoms are not silly, many of us, when anxious, discover that we can at least do one thing to calm down. You guessed it. We can have a drink, a nightcap, or a couple of this or that to "wind down" at the end of the day. A shot, a pill, a snort, before that big meeting, or that speech we have to make, or before the gathering of the bridge club, or that wedding, or that game, or the party, or that sexual encounter, or you name it.

> *. . . many chemically dependent people*
> *use symptoms of depression as a con-*
> *venient "excuse" to use mood-altering*
> *drugs. . . .*

And once we have learned that alcohol or similar drugs "cures" our anxiety over such situations, we are very vulnerable to drinking or using other drugs whenever we experience severe anxiety.

> *. . . resentful alcoholics . . . become*
> *drinking alcoholics, self-pity*
> *becomes . . . potentially deadly. . . .*

PEOPLE WITH THE BLUES

People with the blues may develop many of the same panic symptoms in similar situations. Instead of insomnia, however, some may discover they can't stop sleeping. They can't get out of bed in the morning, and can't wait to get back in at night. At work they feel an overwhelming need for an hour's snooze after lunch. Whereas they once enjoyed family conversation, social affairs with friends, sports, movies, concerts, exercise, now they want to do none of the above.

All depressed persons have difficulty concentrating, remembering, and creating things with words, or cloth, or paint, or any sort of tool imaginable. In time they may find they can't write letters, read the newspapers, or complete simple tasks on the job. Depressed people may slow down and become confused enough to start sentences and forget how to end them. They may open their mouths and discover they cannot remember the simplest words out of their own vocabulary.

Since such symptoms are extremely frightening and make a person feel helpless, he or she may, under these circumstances, be inclined to do almost anything to relieve discomforting symptoms. He may be ready to drink himself into a stupor, thinking that when he wakes up he'll feel better. He may be ready to take a handful of pills or many lines of cocaine in order to change his feelings about himself. People may commit suicide to get rid of depressed feelings so awful they believe they cannot bear them any longer. And since feelings of advanced depression are probably more painful than any physical pain known to man, I suspect that people commit suicide more often for reasons of mental than of physical anguish.

If any person becomes so depressed that he or she can't sleep over a significant period of time, has difficulty concentrating, is constantly preoccupied, feels always fatigued, and has difficulty performing basic tasks or daily work, he or she needs to consult a physician. When depression becomes literally overwhelming, he or she should seek professional help.

In this chapter, however, we address those forms of depression over which we yet may exercise some self-control.

WARNING SIGNS

If you have more than a few of the following feelings, you may be experiencing depression and undue anxiety. Such symptoms are not indications of failure, but a need for support from others, changes in your life, possible involvement in a support group, and, in all probability, contact with a good counselor. If you have alcohol or drug problems, you should talk to a counselor connected with a center specializing in the treatment of addictive disorders.

1. I have difficulty sleeping; if I go to sleep I sometimes wake up with a sudden start.

2. I wake up early in the morning and lay in bed thinking about how bad things are in my life.

3. I have a pervasive feeling that everything is going wrong in my life, and that I am worthless.

4. I feel as if most people I know are doing better than I am in life.

5. During waking hours, I have the feeling that "something is weighing me down."

6. I have difficulty concentrating on what were once simple tasks, activities, or responsibilities connected with my schoolwork, my job, my relationships, or my family.

7. I feel as if life cannot ever be any fun again.

8. I cannot concentrate very well when I read, talk with others, or watch television.

9. I experience panic in situations and places that did not bother me before.

10. I cannot imagine that anyone could possibly love me very much.

11. I have a strong feeling that I have failed in my life.

12. I sometimes wish I could end it all, or that other forces in the world would end it all for me.

HONESTY ABOUT DEPRESSION

We can begin to cope with depressed feelings by simply recognizing that many times such feelings are related to painful problems and memories of the past. Anxiety is generally related to difficult challenges we face in the present or future. Anxiety and depression, in other words, are normal responses to difficult circumstances and uncomfortable feelings.

If we could not experience depression and anxiety we would be subhuman. In fact, symptoms of anxiety or depression become pathological only when they begin to incapacitate us. Even then, the experience may be only temporary. We may not have a specific emotional problem, but rather an overload of feelings we can't manage very well in response to a very stressful situation in our lives.

Many of us reveal our understanding of overload when we say to our friends or family members, "I'm burnt out!" To say, "I'm burnt out," sounds a lot better than to say, "I'm depressed," or "I may be having a breakdown." When we're burnt out, we know that factors outside of ourselves have something to do with our feelings. But we sense, also, that we can do something about them by changing our lives. And if we're not lying or merely trying to cover up our incompetence or laziness, we usually can do something.

When we feel burnt out, however, we must act swiftly and constructively to change that feeling. If we don't do so, we are very likely to begin drinking in an effort to induce a temporary change in our feelings. For an alcoholic, nothing could be more destructive.

COUNTERACT YOUR FEELINGS

When we feel depressed and anxious, we can do all sorts of things to feel better, many of which will counteract our present mood. Please note: when feeling blue or anxious we must often do the opposite of what our mind tells us to do.

Example: when you feel depressed, your mind usually tells you, stay in bed in the morning. You're tired. However, it is usually best for you to get out of bed early, whether you have slept well or not at all. Try to get in and out of bed at the same time everyday, seven days a week. Set times and stick to them. As you set a discipline and stick to it, you already begin to convince yourself that you are not as helpless as you feel.

To gain control over depressed feelings, you need to act against your own feelings. As you grow in a program such as Alcoholics Anonymous' Twelve Steps, you may also draw upon the power of God as you understand Him, to give you the strength to do what you need to do to overcome feelings of depression.

KEEP TALKING TO OTHER PEOPLE

When you feel depressed or anxious and want to stay in your house, try to get out of your house into the fresh air. Though your mind says you need a closed space for protection, you really need open space to free your mind for future possibilities, and for recreation and exercise.

When you feel depressed and anxious and want to avoid all people, talk to people instead. Your mind tells you to think merely about yourself. It's trapped itself into going around and around the same worry track. Since it can't get off the track, it imagines that one more round will surely do the trick. It won't.

Conversation with others will help you get your mind off yourself. As you share your own feelings, or listen for the feelings of others, you will begin to forget your problems of the past, and develop the courage to tackle the challenges of the present and the future. On the simplest level, you may get ideas from other people for coping with your own problems.

When you feel depressed and anxious, plan each day to talk at some length with at least one other person on the phone, at lunch, at work, or around the dinner table. Try to talk with people rather than watch TV. We find that TV often adds to the blues. If we really enjoy watching a program, we may counteract depressed feelings by doing so. If we watch merely to pass the time, however, we will probably increase our sense of helplessness, and become even more anxious.

If you're a recovering alcoholic, or a family member of an alcoholic, and feel depressed, go to at least one AA or Al-Anon meeting a day, and get a sponsor with whom you can talk on a regular basis. A sponsor is someone in AA or Al-Anon with good sobriety and peace of mind, willing to share his or her experiences with others. For many of us, a sponsor has offered a fast way out of the throes of depression and anxiety.

Try to complete the work you know you must get done on any given day. Whatever work you put off makes you feel guilty, and almost literally comes back to haunt you. When you do your work, you convince yourself of competence and power. When you put off your work till the next day, you may convince yourself you cannot do it at all, the next day or any other.

Above all, don't put off responsibilities or engagements, without good cause. Though you may feel better at the moment you postpone or cancel a commitment, you will invariably feel more depressed and anxious afterwards. When you fail to meet an important commitment toward others, you not only feel more helpless than ever, but often guilty about it. And as you feel guilt toward others, you will automatically experience the need to isolate yourself further from them, and thus increase your depression.

Try to complete the work you know
you must get done on any given day.

EXERCISE YOUR BODY

When you feel depressed, exercise your body. Even if you are overweight, you can probably walk out of doors. If you have an indoor exercise routine —aerobics or the simplest pushups or situps—follow it every day. Every adult needs some form of exercise to accelerate his heart beat for a least 12 minutes several times a week. Such discipline clears the arteries, expands the lungs, and offers an invaluable sense of accomplishment and well being.

If you have in the past enjoyed competitive sports such as tennis, golf, racquetball, one-on-one basketball, bowling, softball, try to get back into these sports. When competing against another person, we find it hard to think solely about ourselves. Our desire to win takes us out of ourselves. And when we do occasionally win, we feel less helpless than before.

When anxious and depressed, I've found that success even in one set of tennis "cures" me for a time, and reduces my need to turn for help to a bottle or a pill.

SEX DURING DEPRESSED PERIODS

When you feel down, continue as best as you can, in your present sexual relationships with a mate who already accepts you as you are. Unfortunately, a depressed mind tells the body it doesn't want sex, and for obvious reasons. It feels tired, and is afraid of failure. And who needs that humiliation or embarrassment on top of depressed and anxious feelings?

No matter what our brain seems to tell us, however, we really want sexual companionship with someone "who loves me." Depressed people need love and respect from family members, but are afraid to risk themselves in vital encounters lest they be further rebuffed. Without trying, however, they may never discover whether they are worthy of love and respect from others at all.

Beware, however, of new or experimental sexual liaisons. Failure to succeed sexually with strangers is extremely hard on already depressed egos and conscience. Perhaps most importantly, sexual liaisons at such time carry with them a very high risk for drinking and drug use. Recovering alcoholics often call alcohol "bottled courage." Unfortunately, many alcoholics feel inclined to use bottled courage when they attempt to succeed in a sexual relationship which they know is ill-advised.

EXERCISE THE SPIRIT

When you feel depressed, exercise your spirit as well as your body.

Try to pray, read, and meditate at least three times a day: in the morning when you get up, in the evening when you go to bed, and during at least one quiet time during the day. Pray in positive ways to a God you understand, and who values you positively. Discuss your depression with God and pray for strength. Whenever you can, turn your life into God's hands, as if He had the power to help. To cope with feelings of depression, you need, above everything else, help from a Power greater than yourself. Pray for power positively and God, as you know Him, will give you the power you need. We have learned this in our lives and from the lives of countless other people. Each day try to turn your symptoms over to God, believing He will help you overcome them.

Alcoholism is a physical, emotional and spiritual illness affecting the total person. We recovering alcoholics should try to do something constructive for ourselves in all three areas everyday of our lives. If we say prayers, gather with our AA group or sponsor, and engage in simple exercise every day, we may be positively amazed at how confidently we progress in recovery, challenging depression all the way.

DEPRESSION AND DRUGS

Drugs and alcohol mask feelings and make it impossible for us to change them. If we don't feel them, we won't change them. If we truly want to change, we cannot use mood-altering drugs.

All mood-changers, uppers or downers, ultimately increase the symptoms they at first alleviate. If we take alcohol, tranquilizers or stimulants for an extended period of time to relieve depression and anxiety, we shall for physical reasons alone soon be more depressed and anxious than ever, and further addicted to the drugs we use.

Drugs lead a large percentage of people to dependency and addiction. For most alcoholics, all mood-changing drugs are a potential death sentence.

LIVING THROUGH THE BLUES

God, as we understand Him, has given us bodies and minds able to cope with feelings of depression and anxiety. We can exercise our bodies and minds in the company of other human beings, and be assured of God's presence and strength to live with the past in the present and to face the future. Because God cares for us, and because we experience mutual love and care for other people, we simply do not believe that feelings of depression will destroy us in the end. Because we believe every person has a place in life and something valuable to contribute to others, we know that you can find your own way to live through the blues you experience—without turning to alcohol or other drugs for relief.

A necessary footnote: if you find the suggestions recommended in this chapter fail to help you, then you need to see a physician to gain specialized assistance. When depression becomes deep and chronic, you cannot, without professional help, work your way out of it.

Feelings of depression and anxiety are very common among recovering alcoholics during recovery—especially during the first few months. Most of us alcoholics, however, find that our periods of depression become less frequent and deep as we continue to recover without drugs or alcohol. Hundreds of people, alcoholic and non-alcoholic, have found their way out of depression, over time, by means of constructive thinking and action. You may be one of those who, with God's help, can come up from depression. There is no better time to find out than right now.

Questions For: *Living With The Blues*

1. Why do you think that you have experienced depression? What part do you think alcohol or similar drugs has played in making you depressed?

2. Why do you think so many depressed people use their feelings as an "excuse" for drinking or using other drugs?

3. Depression usually brings with it what alcoholics call the PLOM, or the "poor little ol' me" syndrome. How have you experienced the PLOM syndrome? Give examples.

4. Would you call yourself an "anxious person," or a "depressed person," both, or neither? How does anxiety threaten your sobriety?

5. Why is insomnia a special threat to sobriety and freedom from other drugs? What can you do to combat insomnia?

6. Have you ever had the feeling you didn't want to get up in the morning and face the world? Why is the feeling dangerous for alcoholics and other addicts? What can you do to combat the feeling?

7. Many recovering alcoholics recommend to the newly sober person that he or she attend at least one AA meeting everyday for 90 days. Do you think that might be helpful for you? Why?

9

Handling Sex Soberly

INTRODUCTION

Though it remains a subject difficult to talk about, most alcoholics or addicts create difficulties for themselves sexually by their consumption of alcohol and other drugs. Some alcoholics continue early in recovery and perhaps for the rest of their lives to experience at least some anxiety over their sexual relationships. There is a reason. Sexual experiences and relationships have been and will always remain among the most complex of all human undertakings. It is not surprising, therefore, that persons addicted to mood-altering chemicals should complicate their sexual needs and experiences by altering their moods and behavior through alcohol or other drugs.

This chapter and the next provide a stimulus for honest thought and evaluation of sexual problems which heavy consumption of alcohol may in part create. Though other drugs, both depressants and stimulants, tend to create similar problems, persons addicted primarily to cocaine, hallucinogens, or painkillers (including heroin) may wish to refer to other resources which specifically address the sexual consequences of abusing these drugs.

The persons who have written this chapter and the next, titled, "Responsible Sex for Lovers Only," are members of Alcoholics Anonymous. One of the writers is also a working professional in the counseling field. They are persons who have struggled both with alcoholism and with sexual problems, but have found during recovery a measure of peace and serenity in their sexual lives.

AN APHRODISIAC?

Many us us remember J. Ogden Nash's crude but clever line: "Candy is dandy, but liquor is quicker."

An old English ballad says the same even more pointedly:

"Sherry, my dear? Why yes,
But two at the very most,
Because three puts me under the table,
And four puts me under my host."

Alcohol has long been touted as the lubricant of love, an aphrodisiac. But is it really? Obviously, people down through the ages have wanted to believe so. Even in the present, most drinking people think at one time or another that alcohol increases sexual prowess and satisfaction. There is good reason to think so. When consumed in small doses, alcohol diminishes our inhibitions, increases our sexual desire and confidence, and seems to improve the quality of orgasm.

At first glance, alcohol seems the perfect potion for love. Alcoholics should, therefore, be the world's greatest lovers, the professional sexual athletes among sober but less successful amateurs.

Nothing, however, could be further from the truth. Researchers report that many people who drink large quantities of alcohol actually decrease their sexual desire and capacity for performance. When males consume large quantities of alcohol, they often eliminate their capacity for an erection—hardly an ego boost for the two-fisted drinker. Heavy-drinking women decrease their natural ability to lubricate sexual parts. When drinking heavily, both men and women reduce their capacity for orgasm. They pass out instead. The worst is yet to come.

Alcoholics—those who have lost control over the pattern and amount of their alcohol consumption—may turn themselves through alcohol into sexual failures and social misfits.

Most heavy-drinking male alcoholics lose their capacity and desire for an erection altogether. Since impotency undermines a man's sense of competency as an adult, the impotent alcoholic man feels defeated in every aspect of his life. His impotency becomes a metaphor for complete incompetency.

If chronically alcoholic men continue to drink heavily over a period of years, they reduce their capacity to generate the male hormone, testosterone, and thus shrivel their testicles, develop breast tissue, and render themselves at least temporarily infertile.

And as you might guess, alcoholism is an equal opportunity illness. Researchers find that chronically alcoholic women also experience drastic changes in their sexual behavior and parts, similarly losing sexual desires and the capacity to find pleasure in previously satisfying forms of sexual activity. Over a period of time, heavy-drinking women may cease to menstruate, and may lose their ability to lubricate genital organs by natural means. Thereafter, many become infertile.

The alcoholic circle is completed: alcoholic men cease to be sexually functioning men; alcoholic women cease to be sexually functioning women.

Most discouraging of all: really sick alcoholics don't care any longer how they function sexually, or how other people respond to them. Chronic alcoholics look like a wreck during the day, act like a wreck in bed, and know they're a wreck the next morning. Knowing the truth, they may drown it in the bottle they're hiding, probably under the mattress. Heavy drinking is always a form of sexual suicide—the hardest way we know to give up sex altogether.

Fortunately, heavy drinkers can through abstinence usually reverse sexual dysfunction caused by alcohol—even though it may take some recovering addicts months or perhaps a year to regain physical capacity for sex. When chronically alcoholic people find a way to recover their sobriety, they also begin to recover their sexual ability and their chance for a normal life. That is very important for future peace of mind.

WORRIES OVER SEXUAL PERFORMANCE

In the early phases of recovery most of us alcoholics worry deeply about our sexual performance, perhaps more so than when we drank. And most of us discover ourselves to be initially impotent, or frigid, and just plain scared, even around our wives and husbands. There are reasons for our fright.

First, we'd tried endlessly to have sex when drunk. Now we forget how to have sex soberly. Some of us never had sex at all when purely sober. We always used alcohol or other drugs, as a means to ease ourselves into sexual relationships. Now we don't know how to ease into a relationship without them.

Even, or especially, with our husbands or wives, we find ourselves awfully uneasy. When drunk we didn't care whether our partners enjoyed sex with us or not. When sober we want them to like it and us very much. Worry over the sexual needs of others is, however, a prime sign of early recovery from alcoholism. So try not to worry about your worry.

Though we shall worry in part over our partners' response to our performance, we shall also, even with the first sober try, worry just a little over their sexual enjoyment. In other words we begin during recovery to love our neighbor—our wife or husband—as we learn to love ourselves.

When sober we can begin the way to sexual health, even if we do not function very well at first try. Most of us alcoholics, however, have further reasons for slow recovery of sexual ease and mutual enjoyment with our mates.

THE PAST CATCHES UP WITH THE PRESENT

In stark fear mingled with disgust, many sober spouses for many years may have given into sex with a bleary and bloated physical parody of the person he or she married, but now cannot stand. That bleary and bloated person may have been you.

And in self-disgust and anger, many a drunken partner abuses his unresponsive mate mercilessly with both words and even sometimes physically. Since he knows she despises his condition he punishes her for failing to accept him. That self-disgusted partner may have been you. With similar abandon, female alcoholics often punish their sober male partners.

Why do we act that way when we are drunk?

When taken in small quantities, alcohol diminishes our inhibitions. When taken in large quantities, alcohol eliminates our sense of moral responsibility. The drunken alcoholic, therefore, functions almost like a psychopath without moral concerns for his partner. Obviously, it takes time for our mates to forget our psychopathic patterns of behavior and to return to trusting sexual relationships with us. It takes patience from us to allow our partners to accept our new sober personality.

THE PRICE OF DRUNKEN INFIDELITIES

Furthermore, many an alcoholic and his mate remember infidelities deeply humiliating to both. Since alcoholics do not make the best lovers, some tend to wander around in search of an ego boost through sex. Because they know their own mates find them repulsive, they may cruise the crudest night spots in town, looking for someone who will pretend for a night to find them sexually desirable. Usually, drunken men find similarly drunken women, or visa versa, and prove nothing to themselves except that misery loves company.

Unfortunately, memories of infidelity make for poor communication, sexual or otherwise. With rigorous honesty, therefore, each alcoholic must try to relieve himself of guilt feelings over past wrongs.

If the alcoholic decides to spare his mate humiliation over his own unfaithfulness, he must for good sobriety share his experiences with his AA sponsor, a trusted minister, a counselor, or with an understanding but morally responsible friend. If he does not, his conscience will continue to bother him and perhaps induce him to seek relief from guilt in alcohol.

Some alcoholics try to share their experiences with their mates, often with disastrous results. Not every sober husband or wife really wants to hear details from their recovering spouses about sexual escapades at the local dive! Or with acquaintances from a common social group. In sharing our sexual misdeeds with others, we must use our common sense and thereby try to reduce already hurt and injured feelings.

SHARING ANXIETIES OVER SEX

Because of pride and a sense of modesty, both recovering alcoholics and their mates will naturally try to deny sexual anxiety they experienced in the past and continue to experience in the present. To make progress in sexual relationships, however, they must try their best to share their anxieties.

Though the average person finds sharing of sexual fears difficult, the alcoholic in recovery cannot afford to nurse such uneasiness. Since sexual failure strikes at the root of self-identity, the recovering alcoholic should try to share feelings over past failures with his or her partner. Unfortunately, our sexual failures usually seem far more important to us than they do to others. Our sense of self-importance, therefore, may hold us back from sharing our deepest feeling about sex even with our spouse.

When we began in recovery to speak to our spouses, sometimes humorously, about our sense of sexual failure, we came to realize they loved and wanted us as whole persons, not simply as sexual performers. Actually, they preferred to see us "fail" soberly than to "succeed" drunk.

Above all, we came to realize that acceptance from those we loved would come, but come *gradually,* only in so far as one remained soberly responsible for actions toward our spouses and toward other family members. In your marital relationships, I encourage you to remember, that you did not become for your spouse an irresponsible drunk or drug addict overnight. Therefore, you cannot expect your spouse to accept you as a recovering person overnight either. It takes time. But in time, the God of our understanding can bring about healing for us.

SHARING OUR LIVES WITH EACH OTHER

In order to recover our sexual desires and abilities, we alcoholics and our mates should try also to share the daily events of our lives with each other. Sexual sharing is the foundation of a complex relationship including many physical, emotional, and spiritual aspects. For sexual health, we should try to share with our partner as much of our life as we possibly can. If we have a job, we should for the sake of sobriety and sexual health try to share our work experiences with each other. If we have household duties and children to care for, we can share the work and talk over the responsibilities together.

During my recovery as I regained the simple capacity to talk with my wife about my average days on the job, I also began to rediscover my capacity to share myself sexually without undue fear and self-consciousness. In recovery, we literally get to know each other again as reasonably normal and healthy human beings. When we know each other again, we find that our sexual activities naturally fall into place within the larger relationship.

If we have children, we may have to re-create ourselves as a parent for them. Our drunkeness can have disastrous effects on our children, often driving them to hate and fear the very person they love and depend upon as father or mother. As we try to restore responsible relationships with our children, we also improve our opportunities for mutually satisfying sexual relationships with our spouses.

RETURN TO SOCIETY

To develop an intimate relationship at home, we recovering people must also try to restore or cultivate social relationships with others. As we gain confidence in our conversations with friends and neighbors, we also gain confidence in our sexual contacts with our mates. Fortunately for us, Alcoholics Anonymous and Al-Anon provide great settings for healthy social development.

Sexual capacity depends greatly upon self-esteem and confidence. Sexual self-confidence, however, cannot be created out of thin air by self-inflating talk, or by self-conscious attempts at intercourse. We create it most naturally by succeeding in our work and play outside of sexual activities.

Confidence in our work and relationships translates into sexual confidence with our mates. If we isolate sex from the rest of our social activities and think of it as a performance, we perform selfishly and therefore badly. If we allow sex to fall into place in a larger picture of life, we, in all probability, will function generously and therefore well in time. You may take the word of thousands of recovering alcoholics and their mates.

EASY DOES IT

In sexual relationships, we must constantly remind ourselves that the harder we try to do well, the worse we do. Like sleep, sex is best accomplished when we stop trying to do it perfectly. Let's not take ourselves too seriously in bed. Sometimes, we or our spouse may simply be too tired or not in the mood for sex. After all we do get real headaches from time to time. And normal functioning adults with work and families often have many important things on their minds other than sex.

No matter what the reason, worry over self is always destructive of the self and a symptom of false pride. When humbly willing to accept sexual failure, we shall be less likely to fail sexually. Keep in mind: most sexual failures stem not from illness, but from poor emotional and spiritual habits.

In your daily spiritual exercises, turn your sexual performance together with all other concerns over to God as you understand Him. As in everything else in life, you cannot fully control or manage your sex life. When you turn your experience over to God as you understand Him, however, He will assist you toward mutually satisfying sex with the mate to whom you are honestly committed.

Questions for: *Handling Sex Soberly*

1. How did alcohol, or other drugs, ultimately create problems in your sexual relationships?

2. According to the author, how do many recovering alcoholics recover sexual capacities? What steps will be most important for you during recovery?

3. How will your social relationships with other people help you improve your sexual relationship with your spouse?

4. If while drinking or drugging you were unfaithful to your spouse, what do you need to do to make amends for your infidelity during your recovery?

5. Alcoholics Anonymous has a saying, "Easy Does It," which applies to worry over sexual relationships. Explain how it may apply in your life.

10

Responsible Sex for Lovers Only

INTRODUCTION

In this chapter, we try to help recovering alcoholics find the paths to good and responsible sexual relationships with a spouse or a mate to whom they are totally committed. Single alcoholics looking for romance and a partner may wish to move to the next chapter: "Meeting and Mating During Recovery."

We begin, not with techniques of sex, but with a spiritual and moral basis for sex. With techniques we have discovered how to have sex; with morality we have discovered why. In the process, we have learned how to develop a much happier sobriety through healthy relationships with our spouses.

We write, obviously, about sex with shared, but personal, convictions. Whenever any person tries to write about responsible human behavior, he or she will inevitably express not merely moral preferences or opinions, but also moral convictions. And obviously we know that convictions are always open to discussion and contradiction from others.

As the questions at the end of this chapter suggest, we welcome challenges and even outright "rejection" from our readers. Since we firmly believe neither we nor anyone else can talk constructively about sex without expressing some kind of convictions about responsible moral behavior, we'll take our chances!

To help other addicted people toward a good sobriety of the kind we have experienced in our sex life, therefore, we share our beliefs and urge you to share your reactions with others.

A MORAL BASIS FOR SEX

We may begin to establish a healthy, moral basis for sex by asking the simple question: why do we have sex with our husbands or wives?

One alcoholic has said, "During my drinking years, I thought I needed 'fun' through sex, or release of sexual desire, and often a plain boost to my own ego. In sexual matters, my mind was centered primarily upon myself and my wants.

"In sobriety, however, I wanted something more complex and lasting: an on going sense of unity with my wife, which surpasses any feelings I might enjoy during the act of sex. Though I didn't think about it precisely, I wished for a mutual exchange of unqualified love and acceptance from my wife."

Without at least a measure of that experience, most of us human beings inevitably feel unwanted and incomplete. With it we feel mysteriously or almost "spiritually" complete.

If you have ever felt another person reciprocate your love even on the most tentative level, you have felt the symptoms of that completion. To have sex with the person sharing our love, therefore, becomes one of the physical, emotional, and spiritual attainments for which we have been born!

BEYOND MERE IMPULSE

To enjoy such an experience, however, we have to recognize, we believe, that our sexual desires are not merely impulses to be satisfied but opportunities for mutually gratifying cooperation with the person we love.

If we feel no moral responsibility for that person we shall have no idea what to do sexually with him or her—except to take advantage. We shall insist on gratifying every sexual impulse we experience, and continue, thereby, to create the sexual disasters with which we're so familiar from our drinking or drugging days. What shall we do, then, with those impulses? In one way or another, we sober alcoholics must begin, perhaps for the first time in a long time, to practice self-control over our sexual demands.

And you say, "Oh, no. Not that!"

Don't panic over the possibility of renewed power and control over your sexual life. And don't allow your peers to shame you into thinking that self-control is for wimps. Self-control is for real heroes of recovery. Self-control is one of the keys to healthy sexual experience.

SEX SALESMEN

Unfortunately, many people and some institutions in our society seem to promote the opposite idea almost obsessively: that everything sexual must be good, because it's sexual, and must be satisfied now and not tomorrow.

Some companies, for instance, suggest through advertisements that their products are a sort of aphrodisiac, a means for scoring sexually. Some beer ads portray drinking men in the company of gorgeous women, who hang on their every syllable, and presumably follow them from bar to bed at closing time. Subtly these ads suggest that the purchase of products brings sex as a free bonus. Buy today and have a good time tonight through alcohol and sex. Anything that feels good is good.

As we alcoholics recover our sobriety, we must be careful not to play such psychological games with ourselves. For recovery's sake, we accept moral responsibility for our sexual failures of the past. We insist on the right to claim our own wrongs and our own mistakes, however drunk and sick we might have been. If we didn't feel some guilt about past behavior, we would feel no need to change in the present.

In recovery from alcoholism and addiction, we believe that explanations for our past behavior do not remove our responsibility for that behavior. Rather, they increase our responsibility for the past, and help us work toward happier sobriety through self-control of our sexual impulses in the future.

THE POWER OF SELF-CONTROL

With God's help, we try to practice self-control for good physical, emotional, and spiritual reasons. Healthy sex can occur, we believe, only among people who share the mature ability to judge their own behavior by norms and standards they consider greater than any of their whims of the moment.

Emerson once said, "We gain the strength of the temptation we resist." In the process of controlling unhealthy sexual impulses, we actually acquire in spiritual and moral confidence the power exerted by the impulse. By resisting every helter-skelter impulse for gratification that comes along, we alcoholics learn a new and spiritual way of love and power in life.

People intemperate in sex, work, eating, or consumption of alcohol, always give up their power to that impulse which overwhelms them. By contrast, temperate people are powerful people.

By resisting every helter-skelter impulse for gratification . . . we alcoholics . . . learn a new . . . spiritual way of love . . . .

THE SEX EXPERTS

For the sake of sexual self-control, be on your guard against "sex experts" who say things like, "I do not consider any sexual behavior to be normal or abnormal, proper or perverted, but only acceptable or unacceptable." Perhaps they don't mean what they say. If we believe them, however, we shall deprive ourselves of any serious moral development in our sexual relationships.

Such experts, for instance, may offer recovering alcoholics advice on masturbation. To overcome "negative feelings" we have about the activity, they may tell us to talk encouragingly to ourselves in front of our bedroom mirror, and then to have at it, "freed from guilt." If you ever hear an expert give such advice, however, ask him (or her) when he last practiced what he preaches, and with what result. In this fashion you will begin to discover what the expert himself (or herself) considers normal, proper, and moral.

THE OPTION OF MASTURBATION

In the span of a few generations, spokesmen in our society have shifted from threats of insanity to exuberant promises of health and well-being to those who masturbate. What used to be called "self-abuse" has now become, in the minds of many, an aid toward emotional growth. We seem to have gone from one extreme to another.

Dependent upon our upbringing and current needs, however, we may or may not wish to masturbate. In our experience most married adults find masturbation an adolescent practice over which they feel some sheepishness, and for several reasons.

If experts tell us masturbation is acceptable, our peers during puberty probably told us otherwise. Since the action seems to reflect upon the willingness and capacity of our spouses to fulfill our sexual needs, they feel hurt, dismayed, or disgusted to find us masturbating, especially over nude magazines or romance stories.

Also, since we experience the need to masturbate primarily when we are lonely, anxious, and mildly depressed, we usually don't feel good about it afterwards. There is a reason, we think. If we make masturbation stand in the place of sexual companionship with a partner, we feel less than satisfied, physically and spiritually, with the result. The lonely act of masturbation may remind us of our greater need for sexual companionship with another human being.

SOME THINGS TO CONSIDER

You may wish to reflect upon the following statements. If you identify with the majority of them, you may have allowed sex to become more of a problem than an opportunity in your life. If some of the issues the questions raise bother you a great deal, you may benefit by talking about your feelings with a counselor at a treatment center, or with a therapist who counsels those suffering from both the disease of addiction and with anxieties about matters of sex.

1. I think about sex more than anything else in life.

2. I feel I cannot be a success in life unless I perform well sexually.

3. "Scoring" frequently with different sexual partners is one of my major needs or goals in life.

4. I worry and fantasize a lot about which person(s) I should have sex with.

5. The approval of my performance by my sexual partner(s) means more to me than any other form of recognition I receive.

6. I worry fairly often about becoming sufficiently aroused to satisfy the desires of my partner in sex.

7. I want to gain everybody's attention by being thought of as the "world's greatest lover."

8. I regularly read magazines, books, or watch videos privately, to arouse myself sexually.

9. When I go to parties or similar social events, I always wonder how I can "score" or what person I am going to sleep with for the night.

10. I have a nagging and compulsive need to experience orgasm.

THE ULTIMATE MORAL QUESTION

The moral question we must answer about masturbation, or any other form of sexual activity, heterosexual or homosexual, is simply put. Should we—and do we really want to—do it? Do we consider it right? If we don't, we invariably make ourselves feel guilty through the action, and thus much more susceptible to a slip back to alcohol.

As a simple rule of thumb, we have discovered that the sex we do not wish to share with that person we love the most, we usually don't want to have at all.

---

*Self control is one of the keys to
healthy sexual experience.*

Most normal adults have need for sexual intercourse with someone they respect and love. Because of selfish sexual activities of the past, however, many recovering alcoholics and their sexual partners must learn to trust and respect each other again in order to enjoy intercourse together. The margin for hurt and harm is high in sex. In no other activity in life do we require so much mutual respect and love. Good and healthy sex proceeds from good and healthy social communication through word and actions. As our partners begin to sense that we live not just for ourselves, but for people and values outside of ourselves, they will begin to trust us even in our most intimate sexual activities with them.

FOOLING AROUND

Finally, we approach for some the most sensitive and complicated of sexual issues. If we are committed to another person and have sexual relationships together, just how binding are those commitments? Does such a commitment place other persons sexually out of bounds for us?

With the original founders of Alcoholics Anonymous, we believe absolute fidelity toward wives or husbands is one of the keys both to sobriety and to sexual improvement within a marriage. Lack of commitment to our mates drastically reduces honesty and trust within a relationship, erodes the possibility of healthy mutual sex, and therefore increases the chance for a slip back into compulsive drinking or drugging.

In our view, the last thing a recovering alcoholic needs for spiritual health is an extra-marital relationship. Through such an affair, he will once again fail himself, his mate to whom he is committed, and God as he begins to understand him. An unfaithful alcoholic, will also feel dishonest, and thereby threaten the key to his or her very being: continuing sobriety.

Infidelity creates guilt and ruins spontaneity in sex. If you really want to worry about performance, sleep around. For most of us, infidelity turns spontaneous mutual love into a highly self-conscious performance, often a farce. When we fool around, we place a premium on our own satisfaction and performance. All of a sudden, we've got something to hide and something to prove again. Surely we had enough of such dishonesty during our drinking days.

... the last thing a recovering alcoholic needs for spiritual health is an extra-marital relationship.

WHY DO WE DO IT?

Some recovering alcoholics, however, choose another sexual partner out of pure fear of trying the old relationship with their spouse. In self-pity and resentment, they may assume it's easier—not so much more satisfying as "easier"—to turn to someone else for sex. Very subtly we may also try to punish our mates by choosing someone else—especially if our spouse seems angry and resentful toward us.

But how many of the above do you feel are good and courageous reasons for infidelity? Most importantly: how many of the above reasons for infidelity will help us maintain a happy and guilt-free sobriety?

Based upon the experiences of many fellow alcoholics, we believe that none of these feelings justify an affair—and all tend to soften us up for a slip.

For maximum enjoyment of sober sex, keep guilt, pride, and other self-centered feelings down to a minimum. Good and healthy sex occurs between two people who love each other enough to work and play at it with total honesty together. Among real lovers, satisfying sex simply happens. Expect good things to happen, work lovingly to make them happen, turn the results over to God as you understand him, and some good things will happen. In sex as in everything else, serenity is not getting what you want, but being content with what you get.

WHAT IF YOU DON'T LOVE HIM ANYMORE?

If you think you don't love your mate, or in sobriety suddenly find him or her unattractive, give yourself time, and look again a little later. Don't allow bad feelings early in recovery to ruin your chances for a good reconciliation with your mate. After some months of recovery, many a wife or husband has turned through mutual love into a new and radiant being.

Don't give up the love you already share, however small or fragile, for the whim of the moment, for that gorgeous hunk down the block, or in the AA group. As we understand it, AA is primarily a recovery, not a singles group.

Turn your present sexual problems into God's hands, as you understand him, and things will work out. Give God and yourself time, for your own sake. God and sex are intricately related, though many people, who consider themselves religious, may find the relationship difficult to comprehend. We believe that God made man and woman sexual beings. If God provides the power for alcoholics to recover sobriety, He provides also the ability to recover sexually.

Since sexuality is one of the grounds of our being and existence we may be sure that God, as we understand him, wills our recovery and provides us power and grace for the same. As we turn even our sexual lives into his hands, we already begin that recovery.

Questions for: *Responsible Sex for Lovers Only*

1. When you were drinking or drugging, what did you want from sex?

2. In recovery, many alcoholics want more out of sexual relationships than mere self-gratification. What will you want from your sexual relationships during your recovery?

3. Why is a strong sense of mutual responsibility toward others so important in your sexual relationships?

4. The author says, "The sex we do not wish to share with the person we love the most, we don't really want to have at all." What does that sentence mean to you?

5. Recovering alcoholics often say, "Don't think about separation or divorce from a spouse for at least the first year of sobriety." Why do you think they give that advice?

6. Do you consider sex to be the most important thing in your life? Explain. What things do you think will be equally or more important for you in recovery from addiction?

11

Meeting and Mating During Recovery — A Guide for the Divorced Person

INTRODUCTION

"I gave myself one year to pull myself together, to feel that I was on the upswing and starting, creating, and thinking again," said a divorced woman in her early forties. "And I think I scared myself into believing it, because it was almost one year to the day that I started to see this change in my personality, that I was moving in a more positive direction."

"When I meet a woman and tell her I'm divorced, I've got two kids, and I'm thousands of dollars in hock—can you imagine what happens? Well, I'm at the point right now where I take one day at a time," said a divorced man in his late thirties.

Both of the above speakers belong to the fellowship of Alcoholics Anonymous. As recovering alcoholics who were trying also to survive the shock of divorce, they found in AA a type of support and wisdom they could not easily have found elsewhere.

If you are a divorced person recovering from addiction, you may discover, as they did, that you have unique resources in treatment centers, AA, or NA that may help you cope with the problems of life after divorce.

In this chapter, they will share some of their stories, and some of the discoveries they made together on the road to a healthy and happy sobriety.

WHAT IT'S LIKE–OUR EXPERIENCE

Whenever we meet a newcomer in AA and discover that he or she has recently been divorced, we always feel like asking for a "damage report." If you have been divorced and are also an alcoholic, you know why we want to ask the question.

Whether alcoholic or not, no one who goes through a divorce can anticipate just how it's going to feel after it's over. As we move forward to our final day in court, our anger, resentments, and self-pity seem to sustain us, and even cushion us against the reality of what is going on. When all is said and done, however, we've never met anyone who didn't feel awful afterward. Even alcoholics who are convinced a wife or husband is the "cause" of their drinking feel terrible about the possibility, and above all, the reality of divorce.

After divorce, everything in our lives seems to change overnight. Our children can be negatively affected by the divorce. They may act up and become hard to manage—or so it always seems to us, no matter how hard we try to be a good parent. Half the time, we feel like giving our kids a good spanking and sending them off to bed; the other half of the time, we feel guilty and want to hold them in our arms forever, as if to shelter them against the loss and embarrassment they are experiencing.

If we have a job, a lot of our co-workers suddenly seem tongue-tied around us. We think they're gossiping about our problems. Both single and married people often feel awkward around those who have gone through a divorce. For a while, we don't feel like associating with other divorced people, lest their "condition" rub off on us. For years we thought they were losers, and may somehow have felt superior to them. Now we've joined their illustrious company!

When you go through a divorce, you simply cannot anticipate just how bad it's going to feel . . .

If we have family members or relatives living close by, we discover that some of them don't want to talk about the divorce with us. Even mothers or fathers may snub or reject us. And no matter how well we think we have anticipated the financial crunch of divorce, we don't know until afterward just how tough that crunch can be, especially if we didn't keep the family checking or saving accounts.

LOSS AND LONELINESS

Two things about divorce overwhelmed me more than anything else.

First, though I thought my ex-husband did little for me or for the family, I suddenly "discovered" after our separation a lot of little tasks he had taken care of through the years. I became aware of his absence by realizing, one by one, the simple chores he had done routinely around the house.

He had taken out the garbage, picked up the newspapers off the floor at the end of the day, made salads, helped with the dishes, mowed lawns , cleaned occasionally, and made minor household repairs. Who was supposed to take care of those things now? My children wouldn't help me, at least at first. They did everything possible to avoid taking on any of their father's chores. They acted as if they did not belong to the family any longer—of which I was now the sole head. And I seemed to lack the willpower to force them to work in the house.

Second, I found myself terribly lonely and anxious from the first night of my divorce onward. I began to imagine prowlers around the house, peeping-toms at the windows, rapists in the driveway at dawn's early light. I wanted to get away from the house, but was afraid to leave it. Many nights I didn't sleep at all—or slept only in snatches.

Sometimes when I woke up in the morning, I tried to pretend the divorce had never happened. I kept my eyes shut, and then looked quickly to the other side of the bed to see if my ex-husband was still there. He wasn't. Some days I thought almost obsessively of remarriage—undoing what had been done—but tried as best I could to put the idea out of my mind.

SUDDEN NEW FEARS

Though I am alcoholic and had been fairly active in a local AA group in my town, now as a divorced person I didn't feel like going to meetings anymore. Even when my sponsor called me and told me I had to go to meetings for the sake of my sobriety, I still refused. And I know why.

I didn't want to talk about my divorce with people in my AA home group. When I thought of my married friends in AA, I felt sad. I couldn't yet identify with the women who were divorced. And suddenly, I couldn't seem to face men at all, especially single men.

Dealing with the men seemed to me like going to a dance years ago in high school. The idea made me incredibly nervous. I had been married for about 15 years, had two children, and many married male acquaintances. Now suddenly I discovered that I no longer knew how single men or women acted. How could I go on a date if I didn't know how to act?

> ... *I never made any progress with my worries ... until I started turning them over to God one day at a time.*

Single people seemed too easy going and loose by my standards. They talked with each other effortlessly. Some, but not all, seemed to make spur-of-the-moment decisions to go to bed together, and others lived together in ways that seemed, well, pretty immoral to me.

They had gone through the sexual revolution. I thought I had too, but discovered I hadn't gone very far. Furthermore, I had been faithful to my husband throughout my marriage. Single people, therefore, seemed to have a new morality, while I had an old morality.

THE BIG SLIP

As the days passed, my anxieties increased. If I hadn't had a job to occupy my mind eight hours a day, five days a week, I think I would have started drinking the day after my divorce.

As things happened, one Sunday afternoon about two months after the divorce, I had a glass of wine. I went on to drink a quart, or two (who knows?), of Chablis Blanc, leaving the kids to fend for themselves. Apparently I fell asleep on the living room couch. When I woke it was about 4:00 in the morning, the kids were in bed, and I was scared out of my wits.

I called my sponsor. Being a tough old "bird," she acted as if she was very angry with me, and at 4:00 A.M., undoubtedly was. Rightly, she wanted to know why I hadn't called her before rather than after my first drink. She told me that I had been dumb, arrogant, self-destructive, stupid, stuck-up, and I had better come to a meeting that night, or else. And she knew what she was doing. I got so mad listening to her, that I decided I wouldn't drink that day—just to spite her!

Whenever . . . I had to resolve . . . one of my feelings immediately, I got desperate and wanted a drink.

By 7 a.m., however, I was so scared of drinking some more, and felt so guilty about everything—the divorce, my kids, my mother, my slip—that I struggled off to work, put in my eight hours, and showed up fifteen minutes early for an 8 p.m. AA meeting I had never attended before. That was the beginning of a new sobriety and a new way of life for me.

THE MEETING

The meeting started as if it was going to be a real dud. The speaker for the evening didn't show up. Someone volunteered to lead the meeting, and asked for discussion topics. For several moments, no one said a word.

Then some woman piped up and said, "Let's talk about meeting members of the opposite sex during recovery." And I could have died. Who on earth was this looney-tune? Why was she picking on me?

It turned out she wasn't picking on me. She had also gone through a divorce. But she had attended AA meetings for a couple of months and honestly wanted help. As the discussion developed, I discovered that many of the people present were either divorced or had never married. And the married members went along with the topic.

The man I was later to marry began the discussion by saying, "After my divorce I worried that every woman I talked to wanted to go to bed first, and get married second. I wasn't ready for that."

I could have fallen off my chair. Some single men felt the same way I did about dating after a divorce! I didn't want to go to bed either, and I surely didn't want to think yet about getting married again.

And so the discussion went. Several divorced people spoke honestly about serious difficulties they experienced living as singles. A young, divorced woman told us how she tried to handle herself soberly at parties and at the office around men. All of the people present, I discovered, worried about the same thing I worried about: acceptance from other people, particularly the opposite sex.

SITUATIONS YOU MAY HAVE EXPERIENCED

If you have been divorced and are recovering from alcoholism or other forms of drug addiction, have you experienced any of the following situations? If so, what do you do to cope, retain your sobriety, and continue to work toward serenity?

1. Your children (child) seem after the divorce to blame you for the breakup, and side with your spouse against you.

2. At your office, you enter a room filled with co-workers who suddenly stop talking and have embarrassed looks on their faces. You sense they have been talking about your problems.

3. Your once-close married neighbor, with whom you often gossiped over coffee, now seems unwilling to talk to you about anything except the weather. Or he/she wants to hear all the gory details, which you don't want to talk about.

4. Your mother or father seems unable to admit that your divorce even happened. When you try to talk with them about it, they seem to blame you for the problem, and even side with your ex-spouse.

5. You visit a singles bar, health club, special interest, or support group, reportedly filled with available members of the opposite sex. When you try to talk to people in the bar, club, or group, however, you find yourself almost helpless with anxiety. Without alcohol or drugs, what do you do to cope? Especially if you are in a bar?

THE BEGINNING OF RECOVERY

The highlight of the evening for me came when my future husband said quietly but with wonderful conviction: "To tell the truth, I never made any progress with my worries about future relationships until I started turning them over to God one day at a time. Whenever I felt I had to resolve every one of my feelings immediately, I got desperate and wanted to drink. When I turned them over to God, as I now understand him, I began to realize things would work out for me."

I stared at him as if he had just landed from another planet.

"I couldn't manage my new single life," he said, "anymore than I could control my drinking. I had to turn my will and life over to my Higher Power."

All at once I felt peace of mind for the first time in years. My heart stopped beating so frantically. I heard myself saying out loud, "I needed to hear that. I've been divorced for less than a month, and had a slip last night, because I thought I couldn't go on. And now I don't know what to do. But I want to stay sober."

You could have heard a pin drop.

"You had a slip because you figured you could manage your life again with the help of alcohol," someone said, which made me feel bad again. She was right, though.

With alcohol I thought I could cut down on the anxieties, at least temporarily, and continue to get by. Stinking thinking! With alcohol, I would lose everything I had left: my children, my job, my life.

With God and AA, everything might be possible. With alcohol, nothing was possible. I knew now, however, that things could get better.

A NEW START

After that meeting, someone said to me, "Go to ninety meetings in the next ninety days." I did that. In the process, I learned that my oldest child, a boy, could manage the house for an hour or so, and my two other children would accept his authority—briefly.

Those nightly meetings saved my life. Though I couldn't go out afterward for coffee with the group members, they started coming to my house, and helping me to get the kids to bed and to clean up. Those people cared for me and I cared for them. We want each other to stay sober. We want to learn how to be happy while single again. We need each other.

Off and on I dated some of the men—not my future husband, however. He didn't ask me out, because he wasn't going out with anyone yet. I had some intimate moments with other guys, good and bad. Close companionship came harder.

GOSSIP

When you're divorced and moving into a new society of singles, you may, like me, discover you want to talk about it a lot. And as you see other divorced people, you may talk about them a lot too. You want to gossip! And that can be very harmful for everyone.

When I was gossiping at my worst, I remember reading my meditation book one morning in the middle of July and discovering these words: "Two things can spoil group unity—gossip and criticism. To avoid these divisive things, we must realize that we're all in the same boat. We're like a group of people in a lifeboat after the steamer has sunk. If we're going to be saved, we've got to pull together."

When I was gossiping at my worst, I remember reading . . . these words: "Two things can spoil group unity— gossip and criticism."

What applies to alcoholics applies doubly to divorced and single alcoholics. Gossip destroys confidence within groups and in yourself. When you criticize others, they criticize back. It's like an infectious disease. Once it starts, it's hard to stop.

Why do we gossip about other people's divorces and new relationships? To make ourselves feel better at other people's expense? I wanted to find divorced women who seemed worse off than me. I wanted them to mess up in new relationships they might form. I wanted to keep them away from the eligible men in my group. That's bad business, and destructive of sobriety, and group fellowship. We can't work the steps of recovery if we're trying to hurt someone else. When I stopped doing that—when I decided I was as bad off as anybody else, no better or worse—I began to get better.

ALL THE USUAL DILEMMAS

I know now, I went through the typical phases most divorced people go through. For a while I wanted to give my children back to my ex-husband, or the state. There were times when I thought I just couldn't control them. I bounced between over-protecting and over-neglecting them, sometimes within the same hour. Often, they told me they hated me.

But I kept talking about my problems with other divorced people within the AA fellowship. I learned my family was not much different from any other single mother's family. When I learned to turn over my own children into God's hands, we began to do better together.

For a long while, I hated my mother—or so I thought. She refused to accept the divorce. When she visited, she drove me nuts by pretending everything was hunky-dory. When I finally realized she was denying reality in the same way I had done for years, both with my drinking and my marriage problems, I decided to "live and let live." She still won't talk about the divorce. But I know now it's too painful for her. And I cannot yet do anything to ease that pain.

You can't work the steps of recovery
if you're trying to hurt someone else.

For a month or so, I became strangely convinced I should move back in with my parents. Fortunately, my mother wouldn't talk about that either. My father would have taken me back, I think, largely because he was so wrapped up in his work he didn't care all that much. My mother cared for me enough to say no. She wanted me to survive as an adult in the world. I could not come home again. I could not become her little child again.

HOME WITH THE FELLOWSHIP

Since I didn't go back to my parents, my home became the recovering fellowship of AA. Even my children eventually began to attend meetings of Alatot, and now Alateen. My alcoholism literally made a social life possible both for them and me. We addicted and divorced people have that advantage over the rest of the world.

Gradually, my fears subsided. And one night I asked "Mr. Right" if he wanted to go out to dinner. He said "Not now." So much for Mr. Right. I was really angry at him and myself. A month later he asked me out and stupidly I said, "no," just to spite him. I couldn't believe what I had done. This time I was angry only at myself.

A week later at a meeting we looked at each other and burst out laughing. Both of us wanted to go out together, and both of us were afraid of what might happen. We were unsure of ourselves, and even afraid we wouldn't "perform" very well, as if we were a couple of school kids.

> *"We're like ... people in a lifeboat after the steamer has sunk. If we're going to be saved, we've got to pull together."*

We went out on dates and were strict and moral. We didn't kiss until the second date. And no, we didn't have sex for a long time. Both of us wanted companionship, acceptance, and love from another human being above everything else.

A NEW MARRIAGE

Eventually, we married. And now we share four children together, my home, and a lot of debts. Are we happy? Yes, but not always. But we both have sobriety that has lasted for quite a while. We both attend meetings, sometimes separately and sometimes together.

And each day, we both tell each other we're alcoholic and cannot manage our own lives. And together we turn our will and lives over to the hands of God as we have come to understand Him. We try to live one day at a time as God gives it to us.

All of this has happened because my husband and I "came to believe that a Power greater than ourselves could restore us to sanity," to health, to sobriety, to love, and to marriage. Above all, our Higher Power has given us a basic peace of mind we never had before.

THINGS TO THINK ABOUT:

What are the most important things for a recovering divorced alcoholic to keep in mind day by day? Remember the great AA saying: FIRST THINGS FIRST.

1. Cool it. EASY DOES IT. Things will be bad before they get better.

2. Don't press for new relationships. Don't imagine you have to satisfy every sexual whim you experience from day to day. Try to wait at least a year before you get involved in any complicated relationships, especially those involving sex. Bad

relationships make for bad slips back into alcohol and other drugs.

3. Go to AA or NA meetings as often as possible. Talk with members of your own sex and members of the opposite sex. Get to know the opposite sex socially.

4. At the beginning and the end of each day, turn your will and life over to whatever Higher Power you believe in. Alone, you can't manage. With the help of God, as you understand Him, the fellowship, and the great AA program of recovery, you can do it.

A POSTSCRIPT

Some of the best marriages I know are AA marriages. I don't suggest you plan on one. But if you want to get married again, there's no reason not to hope and pray for an AA marriage.

Just remember, you can't create a marriage, but God can. Turn the problem, however difficult, over to him day by day. Then, growth and change become possible for you. You may yet enjoy a peace of mind you could never have imagined before.

Questions for: *Meeting and Mating During Recovery*

1. Why do you think it takes people so long to begin to "recover" from a divorce? Give examples from your own life.

2. Most divorced persons experience serious loneliness after separation becomes final. Give examples from your own experience. How do you plan during recovery to cope with loneliness?

3. If you have been recently divorced, how do you feel about relationships with members of the opposite sex? Explain. How about close relationships with members of your own sex?

4. Do you feel that members of the opposite sex will find you acceptable? Explain.

5. How do you feel about sexual relationships at this point in your life? Explain.

12

A Time for Family Action— Danger Signs

INTRODUCTION

In this chapter and the next, family members of an alcoholic or drug addicted person will learn how to recognize symptoms of addiction, to disengage themselves from patterns of denial and deception they practice to cover up for the addicted loved one, and to find help both for the alcoholic or addict, and for other members of the family who are dominated by the problem of alcohol or other drug dependence.

Justifiably, addiction has been called a "family disease." The family member suffering from addiction gives out signals of illness, of alcohol and drug abuse. Family members, thereafter, respond to those signals with signals of their own.

Here are some of the typical signals:

1. Worry over a family member's drinking or drug use. The "normal" family rarely worries about social drinking or responsible use of prescription drugs among family members. Worry over alcohol or drug use is usually a sign of problems of addiction within the family.

2. Changes in a drinking or drug using family member's behavior, which cannot be explained by outside causes. The most common changes involve depression, anxiety, irritability, moodiness, withdrawal, aggressiveness, and sometimes the last two in combination.

3. Decrease in the drinking family member's schoolwork or job

performance and a rise in absenteeism, or failure to fulfill common family responsibilities.

4. Reluctance to socialize with friends or relatives. Acquiring a new group of friends whom other family members don't know very well is common, especially for young addicted people.

5. Family preoccupation over the stigma associated with alcoholism and drug use and abuse. Family members begin to deny to themselves and others that there are problems within the household.

When matters have deteriorated this far, a family is in trouble. The following story tells how things may deteriorate further. The writer is a woman in her forties, married to an alcoholic husband. She is presently an active member of Al-Anon.

THE STORY

For many years, I lived with an alcoholic husband, but refused to admit to myself that he had a drinking problem. As a result I put myself and other family members through untold misery.

Because I denied early and obvious signs of my husband's drinking problem, I also came to deny many of the later signs. He ended up drinking himself into a hospital. Meanwhile, I just about went crazy. I hope you won't have to do the same.

My husband is an executive with a large company and typically works a forty hour week. I gradually became aware of his problems with alcohol as he drank more and more both after work and before bedtime. Early in our marriage, we shared a glass of wine before dinner, and maybe another before going to bed. Slowly I began to realize, however, that my husband was no longer drinking with me, but by himself. Often he drank heavily and alone in his study, or silently in front of the TV set. Sometimes he seemed to pass out before going to bed.

> *When is the time for action? Any time you have questions or concern about a family member's drinking.*

My husband had begun to drink in a definite pattern and for unhealthy reasons. He drank not simply to relax or to reduce the anxieties of the day, but to escape from everything for the evening. My husband was "taking a drug"—alcohol—to anesthetize himself before sleep. The next morning he dragged himself off to work, only to repeat the same process the next evening.

If he had been smoking marijuana or using cocaine, I would probably have confronted him and tried to help him stop. But since he consumed alcohol, the acceptable American drug, I held back and hoped that he would somehow quit, or at least cut back on his drinking.

Though I became deeply concerned about him and myself, like the typical alcoholic family member I did not want to believe what was happening in front of my very eyes. Such denial—"not seeing the signs"—comes all too naturally to us family members, because we don't want a drinking problem in our family. Since alcoholism and addiction usually develop subtly, many of us can successfully deny our problems for a long time.

EARLY WARNING SIGNS

Long after my husband had drunk himself into a hospital I learned from hospital staff members and in Al-Alon the early danger signs connected with my husband's drinking.

PURPOSE, PATTERN, AND PREOCCUPATION IN PROBLEM DRINKING

1. Since my husband regularly used alcohol at specific times for relaxation, he came to depend on that drug to wind down at those times. Very shortly, he discovered he couldn't relax in the evening without it.

2. After a while, he discovered he needed more and more of his drug, alcohol, to get the effect he wanted. Gradually he built up both a physical and emotional tolerance for alcohol. He also drank enough to become regularly intoxicated and lose control over his behavior.

3. As he consumed more day by day to relax, he also became preoccupied and vaguely guilty over his consumption of alco-

hol. Before anyone else, he sensed he was becoming dependent on alcohol. He sensed he couldn't sleep, socialize, have sex, or "get the kinks out" of his muscles without alcohol.

My husband was drinking more and more in a definite pattern, for an unhealthy purpose, and becoming preoccupied with his behavior.

BEHAVIORAL CHANGES

When my husband drank, he also began to undergo definite personality changes. When those changes began to occur in my husband's life, I first began to think to myself that he might have a serious problem.

Alcoholics or other drug abusers show the following changes:

1. Some become withdrawn, distant, and seem to lose interest in their work, play, sex, and in other people.

2. Others become hostile and aggressive, and tend to "act out" their angry feelings around other people, especially family members. Some do both. They may also become grandiose.

In other words, addicts and alcoholics tend to become either introverts or extroverts, grandiose or defeatist, depressed or elated. They go to extremes in one direction or the other, and sometimes, dependent upon external circumstances and the state of their health, in both directions.

When my husband drank, he underwent definite personality changes.

My husband was a "home drinker" who withdrew from me and other people when he drank. Later, I learned he felt sheepish about the slur in his speech produced by the alcohol in his system. Instead of talking, he read drowsily or sat by himself in front of the TV set, glass in hand. When I tried to get him to talk with me or our children in the evening, he became angry. If I badgered him, he would take his bottle into his own room and pretend to work. I know now, however, he did little in that room but drink and read *The Rubaiyat of Omar*

Khayyam, and the novel, *The Sun Also Rises,* by Ernest Hemingway. My husband withdrew from me to "socialize" with writers who seemed to justify his drinking.

Though my husband is at heart a sociable person, now he didn't want to go out of the house. When people invited us to dinner or parties, he wanted to stay home. And when he did go to parties, he drank at home before we left, and drank more when we got back. Often, he would literally pass out after the party, fully dressed, on our bed.

When I wanted to invite friends to our house, he put up a terrific fuss. And if I did so anyhow, he drank heavily before and during the occasion, talked very loudly to our guests and often told outrageous jokes. Also, he developed the habit of refilling everyone's glasses, whether they wanted it or not, always making another drink for himself.

After a while, our friends began talking about him privately and avoiding him publicly. Slowly but surely, they stopped inviting us out. Whenever they spoke critically about him to me, however, I became angry and defended him. In fact, I called some of our friends, "Pharisees," and pretended I wanted nothing to do with them—all to protect myself against the thought that I was the wife of an alcoholic.

---

*. . . any time you find yourself uneasy
and worried over a family member's
drinking, you have probably identified
alcoholism.*

Meanwhile, our children became worried that their father would stagger drunk, dressed only in his underwear (or less), into the den when they were entertaining school friends. In time, my children simply refused to bring friends home.

A HORRIBLE THOUGHT

Somewhere along the line in my husband's drinking, a horrible fear struck my heart. Maybe, just maybe, my husband is an alcoholic, which would make me the wife of an alcoholic. My children might have an alcoholic father. My mother might have an alcoholic son-in-law, and so forth.

Then, thinking that a little direct confrontation from me would change him, I challenged my husband's behavior.

"George," I said, "I think you're drinking too much. If you don't watch out you're going to become an alcoholic." That simple challenge produced an extraordinary and unexpected result. My husband exploded.

"If I had a drinking problem, I'd tell you!" he shouted at me. "What do you think I am? Some kind of a skid-row bum? Just knock it off," he said, and seemed ready to hit me.

As some people say, he "blew me away." Husbands and wives learn by instinct how to confuse family members through outrage. Similarly, children with alcohol and drug problems may explode at the mere suggestion they are using addictive chemicals, and try, thereby, to throw their parents off the track.

I decided not to bring up the subject again. I didn't want to think about skid-row any more than my husband did. In a way, I was relieved and satisfied. If he was so outraged at the mere thought of alcoholism, surely he couldn't be an alcoholic.

I was becoming thoroughly confused. And though I needed help badly from other people, I didn't ask for it from anyone—from Al-Anon, from my doctor, or from my pastor. I kept my mouth shut and figured I could manage my husband's drinking for him. In the process, I continued to alibi for him to myself and others.

I covered up for him—among friends, with his employer, and even with our children. I enabled him to keep drinking. And slowly but surely, I began to get as emotionally and spiritually sick as he was. This kind of reaction happens to every spouse and to other family members of an alcoholic—until they seek help.

All of us try to deny the drinking problem in our midst, and cover it up. As things fall apart, we pretend to ourselves that everything will turn out all right. Though day by day we lose power over the drinking and drugging member of our family, we try all the harder to maintain control of the situation. And all of us make ourselves depressed, anxious, fearful, and guilty in the process.

THINGS YOU CAN DO AT THIS POINT

1. Go to a meeting of Al-Anon, the companion fellowship of Alcoholics Anonymous, created and sustained by family members of alcoholics and addicts, and learn as much as you can about living with an addicted person.

2. Call a local treatment center and make an appointment to speak to someone about your family member's problem. Talk to your family doctor or your pastor about the situation in your family.

3. Refuse to enable an addict in the family to drink or use drugs without paying a price for it! Do not purchase drugs for him (or her), serve them to him, store them for him, or give him money for them. You may refuse to make excuses or cover up for your loved one at his or her place of work or school.

4. Suggest to your addicted family member that he visit a meeting of Alcoholics Anonymous in the area. Give him a place and time to attend a meeting. If you have AA literature, make it available to him.

5. Do the best you can to live a normal life at home and at work. Keep up your social contacts with relatives and friends.

VARIETIES OF ALCOHOLIC BEHAVIOR

I have described a little of my husband's drinking habits. Your drinking or drugging family members, however, may have somewhat different habits, different patterns of behavior, and different moods.

My husband was a regular drinker who drank himself into a kind of "coma" almost every night at home. Other alcoholics may sip alcohol or take pills at home, in school, in bars, even at work, and manage to stay on their feet. Some experts call them "plateau drinkers." Though they may continue to function at work and at home, they do lose control over their consumption, and will eventually have the same problems fulfilling responsibilities within the family and on the job as heavier drinking alcoholics do.

Some alcoholics and addicts drink in a binge pattern, often on weekends, on vacations, holidays, and at parties. Teenagers and young adults tend to use drugs and drink in this fashion. To identify a binge drinker, think not of how often they drink, but of what happens when they do. If they repeatedly lose control over their behavior when drinking or using drugs, you may be certain they are addicted to the chemicals they consume.

Some alcoholics drink only at home, others only outside the home. Those who drink heavily away from home usually come in at late hours, miss meals, and forget social events, and family responsibilities. They may regularly mortify sober family members by coming home drunk at odd times of the day and night. When they lose control over their consumption, they may also pose a constant threat to themselves and others through drunken driving.

No matter what their pattern of drinking, most alcoholics can abstain from alcohol or similar drugs for short periods of time. Don't let your drinking family member lull you into a false sense of security with occasional bouts of abstinence—even when you want to believe they are recovering.

Alcoholics use abstinence to prove to themselves and others they are normal drinkers. Normal drinkers, however, never have to prove they're not alcoholic. Therefore, when a drinker tries to prove by abstaining that he is not alcoholic, he usually is one.

Also, if your drinking loved one abstains from alcohol to prove his control over that drug, make sure he does not use a tranquilizer, sleeping pills, or marijuana during his period of "abstinence." And if combined with alcohol, tranquilizers more than double the net effect of both drugs upon the system.

THE VIOLENT DRINKER

Unfortunately, some heavy-drinking persons become loud, overbearing, aggressive, even violent toward a spouse, children, or parents. Usually, your aggressive family members will have more bark than bite. Though they may promise to kick your teeth and the wall in, they may be very frightened of doing so. After violent verbal outbursts, many alcoholic family members become quite repentant, even docile, and will beg for forgiveness.

If a family member becomes physically violent, however, you must find immediate help from other people: from AA or Al-Anon members, from your clergyman, relatives, close friends, or the police.

Violence is not only a red flag sign of alcoholism, but also a signal for early and massive confrontation. For more information about this procedure, you may wish to read the chapter in this book, "Time For Family Action—Victory Through Confrontation."

SNEAKING AND GULPING

Whether passive or aggressive, your drinking or drugging family members will in time begin to "sneak and gulp" alcohol on the side.

By this I mean they will start nipping at bottles in the home, or drink twice as much at the bar as they admit to.

Don't be surprised if you walk into the kitchen or den some evening and find your spouse gulping booze right out of the bottle. It will startle both you and your family member. If you're looking for proof, this behavior ranks as another red flag sign of problem drinking.

. . . your drinking or drugging family member will in time begin to "sneak and gulp" alcohol on the side.

As he sneaks and gulps, your family member may also begin hiding and protecting his supply of alcohol or other drugs. If that member drinks in the house, he or she may hide bottles, pills, pot, or other drugs under the mattress of the bed, in shoes, in dirty clothes bags, in golf bags, handbags, in suitcases and briefcases, in clothes drawers, in car trunks, in garbage cans, under shrubs and bushes, in sofas, over heating ducts in the basement, in Milk of Magnesia bottles, in toilet tanks, in vacuum cleaners, etc. When you expose one place, your drinker will find another.

I have known alcoholics to store alcohol in Windex bottles and squirt it in their mouths. I have known alcoholics to store alcohol in those plastic bottles designed to contain spray for car windshields.

My husband stored small bottles of whiskey in his underwear. He went off to work looking like a ballet dancer in tights.

Alcoholics will drink alone in the bathroom, in the closet, the basement, in the backyard at night, in the car, and in the office during the day. I know an alcoholic woman who climbed into a tree each evening and sipped chablis by the light of the moon. No brie, just chablis.

Away from home, your drinking loved ones will hide bottles in cars, school lockers, office desks, filing cabinets, and anywhere a desperate but clever person can think of. Guilt-ridden drinkers become some of the craftiest people in the world.

As drinkers consume more and more alcohol, most become less and less interested in eating. Beware of the drinking loved one who says he must cut down on food to lose weight. Food diminishes the effect of alcohol on the system. Addicts learn by instinct to avoid food in favor of their drugs.

Some alcoholics gain weight from the calories they consume, especially in beer. Those who don't eat regularly, however, may lose weight, and become slack-skinned and puffy, red-faced and splotchy. Most heavy drinkers also develop problems with blood pressure, digestion, evacuation, headaches, neuritis, hemorrhoids, shortness of breath, and trembling and shaking.

Chronic and excessive alcohol abuse is terribly harmful to the body. It can affect any and all systems of the body, and in time, can damage, if not destroy, them all.

BLACKOUTS

If your drinking family member seems after heavy drinking to forget what he or she has said and done, you are probably witnessing the effects of a "blackout." Large amounts of alcohol affect the drinker's memory. Because alcohol anesthetizes the brain, most alcoholics during a heavy drinking bout "forget" their own words and actions.

When your drinking or drugging family member begins to have blackouts, he is in deep trouble. The failure to remember events and conversations of the previous day may even convince the drinker he's crazy. During confrontation, some alcoholics are actually relieved to discover they have had alcoholic blackouts and not "psychotic episodes."

ALIBIS GALORE

As you might guess, an alcoholic's erratic behavior almost forces him to alibi and lie in order to excuse and explain himself. For instance, if he frequently experiences blackouts, he will try as best he can to fake it—to explain to others why he always forgets what happens when he drinks, or to pretend that he hasn't really forgotten anything at all.

Many alcoholics become experts on wheedling information from others about blacked-out experiences of the previous day. My husband would pretend he remembered conversations at parties, but then craftily interrogate me to find out what he and others had said!

This necessity is maddening both for the addicted person and his (or her) family members. While you may recognize the lies, you may also contribute to the pattern of denial emerging in your own family. Remember: You don't want to accept the reality of alcoholism in your midst any more than the alcoholic does. Thus, you may lie about his drinking as much as he does.

As everybody in the family lies to protect the drinker, the entire family gets sick together. Family members worry that they and their drinking family members will together lose their good name, jobs, status in school, friends, their home and other possessions, all the family has worked and lived for. Everyone feels guilty, angry, self-pitying, and resentful. Everyone thinks the whole world is talking about him or her. Meanwhile, all family members experience increasing difficulty in coping with the problem in their midst.

THE FINAL COUNTDOWN

As fear continues to build day by day, week by week, perhaps year by year, you and your family members may begin to feel that you can trust no one—not even God or your closest relatives. No one will understand your situation, you think. You feel trapped—and humanly speaking, you are.

As the alcoholic loses control over alcohol and his life, so you lose control over the alcoholic problem in your family. And no amount of wishful thinking will resolve your problems. You have to take action. What can you do?

1. You can refuse to help your drinking or drugging loved ones continue. Almost all family members of alcoholics "enable" their loved ones to keep drinking or drugging by purchasing their supplies, protecting them, lying for them, sympathizing with them at the wrong times, and above all, by keeping them away from treatment centers or AA because of selfish concern over stigma.

I did all these things and you may be doing them right now. But with the help of Al-Anon and a God, as I now understand Him, I finally stopped enabling my husband in his drinking. You can do so also with your family member.

2. You can act. When is the time for action? Any time you have questions or concern about a family member's drinking. At any point you suspect your family member has problems which you realize you cannot manage or control. When you find yourself overwhelmed with anxiety and fear about your life and the future of your family.

3. When you want help from others, where should you turn? Look into your phone book and try to find the number of Al-

Anon. If you wish, you may ask for someone from Al-Anon to call or visit with you to describe the Al-Anon program. If no Al-Anon number is listed, call the AA number and ask for information about Al-Anon meetings in your area.

. . . no amount of wishful thinking
will resolve your problems. You have
to take action.

---

4. You can also call the information referral service in your area, or call your local treatment center for help. Treatment centers are usually listed in the Yellow Pages under "Hospitals," or "Physicians," or "Alcoholism." If you cannot find information through your phone book, visit with your pastor or doctor. In all probability, one or the other will know of Al-Anon groups and treatment centers in your area.

Al-Anon is made up of family members and close friends of alcoholic and addicted people. Al-Anon members gather in weekly meetings to gain insight and strength for recovery and for spiritual growth— whether their family members are still drinking or not. Al-Anon is for you, the family member. The Al-Anon program will help you recover from your own problems of body, mind, and spirit.

5. If you are an active member of a congregation or synagogue and trust your clergyperson or rabbi, make an appointment and share your concerns and feelings with him or her. Many clergy today receive training in the counseling of alcoholics and family members, and may be able to help you when you or your drinking loved ones seek help in a treatment center.

6. If you have close friends or relatives familiar with drinking and drugging problems, you may benefit by talking honestly with them about the realities developing within your own family. When you bury your fear and anger over the alcoholic in your house, you hurt yourself. As you begin to share your problems with Al-Anon members and other people, you will begin to detach yourself from the problems of the alcoholic,

and learn from others how to regain a measure of control over yourself and find a new way of life.

Unless you seek help from Al-Anon and other people, however, you will continue to deteriorate and perhaps eventually break down under the weight of your problem. Unless you are able to turn your problems over to a Power and people stronger than yourself, hopefully to a God you come to understand, you could either leave your loved ones or lose them, and certainly lose also a part of your self.

CONFRONTATION

Finally, I strongly encourage you to counsel with an experienced professional person—a treatment center counselor, a doctor, or a minister—in order to learn how to confront your addicted loved one with the reality of his or her problem and so induce him or her to get help through treatment and AA. Unless you and other family members do something to confront your addicted family member about the necessity for help, he or she will continue to deteriorate. Alcoholism and other forms or addiction are chronic, progressive, and fatal illnesses which may be arrested.

With the help of others, you can begin to prepare yourself for confrontation with your drinking or drugging loved ones. In the next chapter, *A Time for Action, Victory Through Confrontation,* I will describe the techniques of confronting a family member with the reality of addiction, and helping him or her into treatment and recovery.

Questions for *A Time For Family Action—Danger Signs*

1. When did you first begin to worry about your family member's drinking or drug use? Describe your experiences.

2. The author of this chapter feels that she began fairly early in her husband's drinking career to exhibit many of the same "sick" symptoms of behavior that he exhibited. Did you have similar experiences as you tried to cope with an addicted family member? Explain.

3. All family members of alcoholics or drug addicted people become fearful and anxious about the future. Describe your experiences with fear and anxiety.

4. The author's husband regularly drank too much and got drunk. Other drinkers or drug users may drink or use other drugs just enough to keep themselves perpetually high, or drink in binge patterns on weekends, holidays, or at parties. In what pattern did your family member drink?

5. Do you believe both your loved one and your family members can get better in the future? Describe your feelings.

13

A Time for Family Action— Victory Through Confrontation

INTRODUCTION

In the previous chapter the wife of a recovering alcoholic described many of her failures in trying to cope with an addicted family member. As the writer indicated, however, many of her failures might have been prevented had she known more about the nature of addiction, and the ways in which addicted people can be confronted about their illness and encouraged to seek help for recovery.

In this chapter, another woman and wife of a recovering alcoholic describes how and why family members tend to "get sick" along with the alcoholic or addict in the home. The writer then presents ways in which the family may confront a sick fellow member and help him or her to treatment and recovery.

A FAMILY ILLNESS

I am the wife of a recovering alcoholic. Though my husband has not had a drink for some time, he drank heavily for many years, and brought untold hurt and harm upon himself and upon his family members.

As my husband drank, I also deteriorated to the point where I needed help for myself. Because I loved him deeply, and did not know how to help him, I followed him—with about the same symptoms of illness—into the quagmire of addictive disease.

Though I didn't drink I did, however, begin to act and sound like my drinking husband. If you have a drinking spouse or other family member in your home, you will probably also develop many of the same symptoms he or she exhibits. That's why experts often call alcoholism a "family illness." Since most family members begin to mirror the symptoms of their addicted loved ones, the problem of common symptoms becomes fundamental both for an understanding of the family concept of addictive illness and for its treatment.

I want to begin, therefore, by discussing this diabolical predicament. How do family members get as sick as their drinking or drugging loved ones? What happens? Why?

WHY FAMILY MEMBERS GET "SICK"

1. Minimizing the alibis. On the most elementary level, an alcoholic or addicted family member always tries to minimize and excuse the effects of his consumption of mood-altering chemicals. If the alcoholic has a family, for instance, he will constantly create alibis to "explain" away" his failures to fulfill family responsibilities.

An alcoholic housewife, when drunk, may be unable to cook the simplest meals or clean her home, but will pretend to family members that sinus problems, or constant headaches, have incapacitated her. Similarly, alcoholic men may blame their inability to mow the lawn, prune the shrubs, or tackle home repairs on that ol' bad back, trick knee, migraines, the office "grind"—especially the overbearing boss who never "gives him a moment's peace"—and, on his wife. Both alcoholic men and women become experts at tracing their erratic behavior back to their jobs and/or to their spouses, or other family members.

2. Guilt and fear. In the process of alibiing for irresponsible behavior, the alcoholic in your family experiences constant guilt and fear, and becomes terribly worried about the future. Though he doesn't really want to lie all the time, he cannot figure a way out of this trap— without giving up his alcohol or other drugs. However, as an alcoholic drinking out of control, that is precisely what he cannot do by himself. He finds himself, therefore, in an almost unbearable "Catch-22."

The lying alcoholic pays a price, but so do the family members. Because we spouses hope with every fiber of our being that our family members are not really alcoholic, we also tend to minimize the sheer amounts of alcohol or other drugs they consume from day to day.

3. Lying and manipulation. Though we are shocked by their be-

havior, we pretend to ourselves it isn't all that bad. Or we may secretly enjoy the chance to try to manipulate the alcoholic in our life, to control our family members, and our personal affairs. But since we don't want people outside the family to know about our loved one's drinking, we simply refuse to be honest about the problem to ourselves, to other family members, and to our friends. We lie to ourselves and others. And as we lie, we also feel guilty, depressed, and become gradually sick at heart.

Even if our drinking or drugging loved one begins to lose his health, we may still hide his real problems from those who could help him the most. I once took my husband to a local emergency unit of a hospital for a "heart attack," which I knew resulted from his consumption of an entire quart of bourbon one night when he was supposedly "watching television." The "emergency doc" wanted to hospitalize him for alcoholism treatment, but I insisted the binge was merely an isolated "accident"—the result of a family reunion party, which I made up to cover for my husband's behavior.

4. Anger and anxiety. If we family members continue to cover up for our family member, we also begin to suffer from pangs of conscience, fear, and from overwhelming anger. Unless we learn to confront him with the reality of his illness, however, we shall take our feelings out on ourselves and other family members. And when we do so, we fail to give our non-alcoholic loved one even that measure of true comfort and support he needs. As a result, we all get confused and disturbed together.

Whereas we once may have slept soundly, now we find we can't go to sleep, or we wake up every hour with a start, or wake up early, and can't go back to sleep, or all of the above. Because our worry over the future gradually becomes pervasive, we simply cannot function normally any longer during the day or night. Like our alcoholic family member, we have difficulty concentrating even on many simple tasks at the job or in the household. If we have paying jobs, we begin to miss work because of "nerves" and lack of sleep. Then we begin to alibi for our own absenteeism.

5. Loss of faith—worry over stigma. Once, we may have had healthy and sustaining relationships with a God of our understanding, and with a church fellowship. Now, in our depression and anxiety, we discover we can't pray because we seem to have lost faith in God. And we may not wish to worship any longer in our church, lest others find out about our problems and think us hypocritical.

On top of everything else, we constantly worry, for good reason, about the stigma associated with alcoholism. Regardless of what you read in the newspapers about society's acceptance of alcoholism as an illness, many people still understand little about it, and talk about it as a moral failure of considerable dimensions.

Since we don't want people in our social group to know about our developing family problems, we gradually cut ourselves off even from close friends. We may even find ourselves forced to lie to our closest relatives. Since my mother was never "sold" on my husband, I defended his behavior tooth and nail, and as a result almost severed my ties with a parent I dearly loved and depended upon.

6. Medical treatment. Somewhere along the line, I went to my own doctor, talked about anxiety, depression, and insomnia, and received both sleeping pills and tranquilizers for my symptoms. Though I hated drugs, I was now using them to cope with my own feelings! Because I felt ashamed, however, I told no one I was doing so. Our family, therefore, became a regular drug store, with everyone sneaking and gulping his or her favorite chemical off in a corner somewhere.

I reached the point where I literally felt both hopeless and helpless about my past and future. No longer was I primarily concerned about my husband's problems. I now had more than enough of my own.

THE TERRIBLE TEMPTATION TO ENABLE

If you happen to be in a position similar to the one I have described, you know how hard it is, even when you experience great emotional pain, to confront your loved one and say, "Go in for treatment or get out of here." "Go to an AA meeting or I'm leaving." "Get help, or I'm calling your boss."

> . . . *we constantly worry, for good reason, about the stigma associated with alcoholism.*

I have a friend in Al-Anon whose husband was a drinking dentist. Every day she feared that he would drill a hole in one of his patient's gums, or cap the wrong tooth. Every day, she expected the phone to ring and to hear that her husband had been arrested for injuring a patient. Yet, day after day, year after year, she did nothing, until finally he seriously hurt a patient, lost his license, and later committed suicide.

Why did he keep on practicing dentistry even when he was drunk? In part, because his wife enabled him to do so. How? By failing to confront him with the realities of his illness. Why? Because she was afraid of hurting herself by making him and others aware of the depth of his difficulties.

I know this sounds dreadful, but she would be the first to admit that it is true. When we family members fail to confront our loved ones with their problems, they will continue to get sicker. If we don't detach ourselves from the havoc our drinking family members cause us, we will not only participate in that sickness ourselves, but become part of it.

For instance, I spent so much time whining, needling, and nagging at my husband to do something about his drinking, that my own children finally became justifiably fed up with me. Frequently, our teenage daughter would tell me, "Mom, you're ten times worse sober than dad is drunk." And she was right. We may think we have every right to our frustrated behavior, but our feelings don't make us any more likeable around others.

When finally I began to attend Al-Anon meetings and learned how to detach myself emotionally from my husband-problems, while still loving him, I also became much more lovable around my children and my friends. To become lovingly detached from your drinking family members, you must also stop enabling them to drink.

A TEST FOR YOURSELF—ANSWER "YES" OR "NO"

1. I have worried more than once about a family member's drinking or drug use _____.

2. I have been embarrassed more than once by the behavior of a family member who was intoxicated with alcohol or other drugs _____.

3. I have offered excuses to other people in order to "explain" or cover up for a family member's behavior when intoxicated _____.

4. I have felt hurt or worried when a drinking or drug-using family member made new "friends" at parties, bars, or other places, where alcohol or other drugs were used socially _____.

5. I have more than once thought, with a sense of shock, that a family member might be an alcoholic or drug addict _____.

6. My own emotions and health have been affected by the drinking or drug use of a family member _____.

7. I have worried about the possibility of other people learning about the drinking or drug problem I have in my own family _____.

8. I find myself angry both at a family member who uses alcohol and/or other drugs, and at others who suspect that he or she is using _____.

9. I have found evidence, such as hidden bottles and prescription drugs, "street" drugs, or drug paraphernalia, which indicate a family member is using alcohol or other drugs secretly in the home _____.

10. I sometimes feel completely helpless and full of fear about my own and my family's future _____.

If you answer three of the questions with a yes, you probably have an alcoholic or addicted family member in your home.

A WAY TO RECOVERY: AL-ANON

To learn about loving detachment from addicted family members, I first and foremost recommend that you attend Al-Anon meetings in your area, and, if possible, speak to a counselor in a family program connected with a treatment center.

If you can get to a town with even a few thousand people, you will find Al-Anon groups. Al-Anon is the companion group to AA, for family members of alcoholics, drinking or sober, and follows a recovery program similar to that of AA, but tailored for non-alcoholic people.

To find out about meetings of Al-Anon groups in your area, check your phone book for Al-Anon or an Alcoholics Anonymous phone number. Call and ask for a schedule of weekly meetings. If you belong to a congregation, you might ask your pastor or rabbi for information. Some doctors are also familiar with the schedule and program of AA and Al-Anon groups in their areas. Some doctors in your area may belong to AA or Al-Anon, and can be especially helpful to you.

If you wish, Al-Anon will often send out a member to speak to you about its program of recovery for family members. That Al-Anon member will be the loved one of an alcoholic or addicted person. She or he could in time become your "sponsor," a person with whom you can talk any time you feel you need help with your own problems.

Al-Anon meetings cost nothing, and are often held weekly in donated church facilities. When you attend a meeting, no one will pressure you to speak even one word. You may simply sit and listen, and if you wish, talk afterwards to Al-Anon members. And since Al-Anon members agree to reveal nothing about who attends or what is said at a meeting, and use only first names, no one outside that group will ever know you attended.

Al-Anon offers no plan of recovery for your drinking family member. That family member must find his or her way into AA. But Al-Anon guarantees you physical, moral, and spiritual support and strength. If you follow the Al-Anon program, you are bound to feel better, and gradually learn to detach yourself, with love, from the problems your loved one is experiencing.

INTERVENTION

Once you have begun to detach yourself emotionally from the problems of your loved one, you can learn from professional staff members of your local treatment center and/or experienced Al-Anon members how to confront the alcoholic in your family and induce him or her to seek treatment.

Confrontation, or intervention, allows family members, and other concerned persons such as employers, to share openly and honestly both the facts about the alcoholic's behavior and their emotional reactions to that behavior.

The intervention process often consists of the following. Family members of the alcoholic person, plus hopefully an employer or fellow employee, and perhaps a pastor, a doctor, or treatment center counselor close to the family, literally confront the drinker both with the evidence of his or her alcoholism and with the need for treatment. The intervention "team" must try to convince the drinking family member that he or she needs help.

Intervention works best when all members of the team are convinced that the troubled family member must have treatment for a chronic, progressive, and fatal illness.

Intervention works best when the "team" consists of close family members who know intimately of the drinker's pathological behavior, an employer who can remind the drinker of a possible loss of job, and a trained professional who can substantiate on a scientific basis the acute need for treatment.

Not every intervention team contains all these components. You may have difficulty finding a knowledgable and willing pastor or doctor, especially if you have no church ties. Your family member may be the boss of his company or a professional himself, which makes it difficult for him to accept professional advice from others. However, it is usually advisable to seek the assistance of a trained alcoholism counselor when planning an intervention.

THE PLAN

Many intervention teams plan a simple get-together with the drinker in the house, or in a neutral place. At an appropriate time, however, one of the family members must tell the drinking loved one the real reason for the get-together. And when the drinker inevitably complains, perhaps weeps, wails, and gnashes his teeth, at the skull-duggery of his family, the family must hold firm. Treatment is needed.

When the alcoholic says he will shape up tomorrow, the family members must say, "We know you mean well, but we know also you can't shape up without help from others." When the alcoholic says, "My drinking's not really all that bad," family members must be prepared to give recent examples of his behavior.

Let the alcoholic in your family know how often he gets drunk, how often he isolates himself, or abuses others when drunk, how often he has missed work, how often he has passed out in front of the TV, or fallen on the floor instead of the bed to sleep. Let the alcoholic know that his close friends or fellow employees don't want him at their social affairs any longer. Let him or her know that you can no longer invite anyone to the house for fear that the drinker will embarrass himself and others with drunken behavior.

No matter what he says, keep the facts before his eyes. Let him know that he can enter a treatment center right then. This is particularly important. Talk to a treatment center admissions person before the confrontation and, if possible, get someone to plan the confrontation. In the process, you can assure yourself of a room for your loved one in a treatment center.

Tell your family member that treatment programs usually last 28 days, and provide continuing daily education, individual counseling (including recovering alcoholic counselors), group therapy, physical therapy, medical care, and good, healthy social interaction both with fellow patients and staff members who understand alcoholism and other forms of drug addiction.

No matter how angry or remorseful your family member becomes, you must stick to your guns and insist upon treatment. If necessary, you may have to separate yourself from your addicted family member, if he or she does not seek treatment. This is your way of letting the alcoholic know that his actions and condition have produced a crisis for others.

TOUGH LOVE

Most alcoholic people begin to think seriously about treatment only when they realize they risk devastating consequences for failure to do so. Though ultimatums sound cruel, they serve as a healthy reminder to the alcoholic that, in the language of the First Step of the Alcoholics Anonymous and Al-Anon programs, he or she has become powerless over alcohol; life has become unmanageable.

If your family member had cancer and denied the need for treatment, you would confront him or her and force the issue. Alcoholism is also a progressive and fatal illness. Surely you and other members of your family want to help your loved one overcome his need for denial. You may have to show "tough love" in order to provide him or her help.

When confronted with the possibility of separation from family and job loss, most alcoholics will choose treatment in an inpatient facility specializing in addictive disorders. Though your loved one may enter treatment angry at you, and deeply depressed over himself, he will after treatment probably feel grateful for your help, and realize that intervention was evidence of your deep and loving concern for him.

If you confront your drinking family member successfully, you may literally save his or her life. As you prepare for confrontation, keep that foremost in your mind!

WHAT NEXT?

Your alcoholic loved one may or may not enter treatment and AA, stop drinking, and begin recovery. Much depends upon his or her incentive to accept help and to get better. The more the alcoholic has to live for, the more likely he will recover. Loving family members and satisfying employment are some of the most important factors in recovery from addiction. When you stick by your drinking family member, you make it much easier for him to enter a process of recovery.

I strongly encourage you, however, not to make your own health contingent upon the recovery of the drinking or drugging member of your family. So many people in so many troubled families literally fall to pieces because they cannot learn to detach themselves physically, emotionally, and spiritually from the disease of addiction within the household.

If you find you cannot detach yourself from the problems experienced by your addicted family member, you may require special help in order to regain your stability. For that reason, I cannot emphasize strongly enough your need to share your problems regularly at Al-Anon meetings.

If you still have difficulty, seek out professional help at an alcoholism treatment center in your area. These centers provide consultation opportunities, programs for family members, and afterwards will offer you regular counseling sessions, which may be covered by your insurance program.

With the help of God, as you understand him, and the help of sensitive people in Al-Anon, you can learn to live comfortably with a recovering alcoholic, and even with a drinking alcoholic. But you must choose to seek help.

MY NEW LIFE

I am one of the fortunate people in Al-Anon who can say today that my husband is sober, healthy, and productive. Since he has stopped drinking and become an active member of the AA fellowship, he has literally become a person I hardly knew before.

When we first met, my husband was drinking socially. And though the alcohol affected him only marginally, he was already on the way toward dependence upon that drug. Already, he was feeling vaguely guilty about that dependence, irritable, and hopeful of stopping someday.

Now that he has stopped, he is infinitely more cheerful, benign, loving, and considerate of me, our children, and of other people. Our old friends seem to enjoy his company at our common social gatherings as they never did before. And we have dozens of new and close friends active in the AA and Al-Anon fellowship.

I am not inferring that either he or I has achieved perfection. As the AA Big Book says, none of us are saints. Under pressure, we still lose our tempers, fight with each other, or anger friends and acquaintances with thoughtless or brusque remarks. I often experience a strong desire to manipulate and manage his life as I was forced to do when he was drinking—a common problem among spouses of recovering alcoholics. But, afterwards, we are always aware of our failures, often share them, and resolve together to try, with God's help, to do better. We seem, each day, to grow in emotional and spiritual strength.

You have every reason for hope, so long as you are willing to ask for help.

As strange as it sounds, my husband and I can both say now that we are grateful, almost happy, that we have gone through this experience together. Without it, we would have remained simply self-centered, self-pitying, and resentful, like so many other people we know in our world. Today we find ourselves remarkably free from the domination of those destructive feelings, and able to give and receive love so much more easily.

THERE IS HOPE FOR YOU

If you find yourself presently struggling in the "valley of the shadow" with a drinking or drugging loved one, I can assure you that the best may yet come your way. But you have to act.

If you really want help, call Al-Anon or AA now. Contact a treatment center in your area. Pray for help, muster your courage, and do something. And I can almost promise you that things will go better for you in the future. You have every reason for hope, so long as you are willing to ask for help.

Try it. You have nothing to lose but your pain.

Questions for: *A Time For Family Action—Victory Through Confrontation*

1. Did you feel the need to hide the problems of your addicted family member from the rest of the world? Describe your feelings and experiences.

2. Most family members actually "enable" their alcoholic loved one to keep on drinking or using drugs. Explain what the word "enable" means in this context, and how you may have enabled your loved one to drink or use drugs.

3. Have you resorted to alcohol or mood-altering medications for relief from your own anxiety or depression? What are the dangers of such efforts to find relief?

4. Have you ever been to an Al-Anon meeting? Does Al-Anon appeal to you? Explain.

5. Have you confronted your loved one over his or her drinking or drug use? Describe your experience. Why is professional help—especially from a treatment center—usually necessary for an effective confrontation of a drinking or drug abusing family member?

6. If your family member fails to recover and remain sober and clean from drugs in the future, what is your plan of action for continuing health and stability?

14

Young and Restless—For The Young Person

INTRODUCTION

The writer of this chapter is a 22-year-old recovering woman named Holly. She is unmarried, an accountant in a hospital outpatient department. Early in her life she became physically and emotionally dependent upon alcohol and a variety of other drugs. With the help of a treatment center and the recovery programs of Alcoholics Anonymous and Narcotics Anonymous, she has remained "straight"—dry and clean—for a year and a half, and is moving forward with serenity and dignity toward a sober way of life.

If you identify with her, we hope her story will help you to seek sobriety, continuing recovery from alcoholism and addiction, and the happiness which comes with a better life.

EARLY YEARS

As I thought about writing about my first serious experiences with alcohol and drugs, I found it hard to be honest and truthful with myself. Why did I start using in the first place? Why in a small town in upstate New York did so many kids in junior high or early in high school decide that cigarettes, alcohol, and pot had to become "rites of passage" for them to adulthood? Or did we all just try to have a good time by drinking and using drugs? To rebel against our parents and teachers?

Were we bored, restless, and unsure of what we were supposed to do in life? I think it's a combination of the above.

Addicted persons and therapists sometimes blame "peer pressure" for kids' use of drugs. That phrase, however, is hard to define, and may tend to take responsibility away from young users themselves. In reality, kids simply decide together to drink beer and use some of the other mood-altering chemicals for "a good time." We pressure each other to have the experience and prove to ourselves that we can have fun.

Most of our parents didn't want us to use alcohol or drugs—at least on our own. Most of us kept our drug use a dark secret from all adults, and even from some friends our own age. And when adults began to catch on to what we were doing, we denied our use with such outrage that they backed off. They wanted to believe us.

No boy or girl ever twisted my arm and said, "Holly, drink a beer, or I'm going to hit you. Smoke that joint, or I'm going to rearrange your face." For all I remember, I may have been the first in my crowd to use. I think, though, that some of the boys began drinking, and smoking a little pot now and then, and I followed suit.

We all wanted to impress each other. We wanted to do something wild and crazy our parents didn't know about—something illegal, against school rules, and against "society." Though we were afraid of being caught, the joy of putting something over on adults was half the fun.

I am one of those alcoholics who liked the effect of the first beer I ever drank. I was about 12 or 13, and had always been shy, not terribly good-looking, a little tongue-tied, and convinced that no boy would ever give me a second glance. I had a few girlfriends, and we all thought, without even talking about it much, that we were losers.

> *. . . we all wanted to impress each other. We all wanted that feeling . . . of doing something our parents didn't know about.*

But that first beer changed my entire attitude toward myself! All of a sudden I felt good about myself and attractive and sexy. Suddenly, I could talk to boys and make them laugh. When I drank or smoked a joint, boys seemed more interested in me. I believed that drinking that bottle of beer was the first day of a new life for me.

ON EASY STREET

For a while it worked that way. When I was 14, I was already "going steady" with a tall, skinny boy with pimples, a little fuzzy moustache, and a motorbike. He drank like a fish, smoked pot every day, and gave me my first pills. He said they were "reds," and he bought them at a local bar where small-time dealers hung out.

We fumbled our way into sexual intercourse, which for me was a kind of silly experience the first time. I was too nervous to have any real sexual reactions. The boy talked as if he were a sexual veteran, but I think it was his first time too.

Like a immature teenager, I bragged about if afterward with my girlfriends. The moment I lost my virginity, I acted as if the earth had moved. I made up all kinds of details just to make the experience sound more interesting to other girls. All of us overrated our experiences with sex and drugs in order to show off around each other. That's a key to our early drinking and drug using: showing off.

YOUNG PEOPLE WHO GET HOOKED

Most young people like myself who get hooked early on alcohol and drugs are insecure and lonely. We don't have a lot of close and loyal friends, especially among the other kids at school. Usually, we don't get along very well with our parents or teachers, and we criticize them endlessly in each other's company. We're very cynical and critical about everything and everybody.

That's very important for understanding young addicts. We think we don't like our parents, their way of life, or the world they live in. We don't want to grow up to be like them. Maybe our parents are cruel to us: abusive, heavy-drinking, or really crazy people. We may have to isolate ourselves to stay out of their way. We may have to run away. But if we do, where are we going to go, and who are we going to use as role models for the adult life?

ROLE MODELS

When you are 14, you usually have little idea of what you're supposed to do with your life. You just want your life to feel better than it does. You want people to like you and praise you. And when you feel depressed and rejected, you learn quickly that you can change your mood with alcohol or drugs.

Also, you look around in school or the neighborhood and you see wild and crazy kids, using drugs and partying a lot, and you see straight kids who go to church and 4-H clubs, or scouts, others who get straight A's; you see nerds and kids who stay home and probably read books. And over a period of time—it could be a day or week or month—you make a decision between belonging to one group or the other.

The wild kids drink and use drugs. The straight kids don't use very much. At parties they may have a couple of beers. But they don't get wasted. They don't fall down a stairwell and break an arm the way I did at a party one night. And they don't seem to have a lot of sex; maybe they don't have any. But since all the wild kids are having sex, you feel pressure to have sex too, both for the experience and for the status.

> *Most young people who get hooked early on booze and drugs . . . are incredibly insecure.*

Sex and drugs can go hand in hand. When you're using drugs heavily, you think in the back of your mind: I'm going to find the right guy and have really good sex pretty soon. Danny is really gonna like me. He's high and I'm high.

Boys may be more interested than girls in simply having an orgasm. They're more interested in scoring and bragging about it afterward to other boys. Most girls want close relationships with boys, which they can analyze and brag about to other girls. But girls want orgasms too, and want to brag about them also to other girls.

A lot of young girls really want to make it with "important guys." Why do you think some girls go bananas over rock singers? Always we think someday we'll make it with a star, and then afterward, tell the other girls about it. Girls want the security and status that comes with having an important boyfriend. And everybody wants to brag about it. Drugs and the sex are a means to an end: competing with members of your own sex. There's not a whole lot of difference between boys and girls. Don't let anyone confuse you on that score.

At 14 . . . You feel depressed and terrible, but learn you can change your mood with booze and drugs.

LOSING CONTROL

Now, all of this might turn out to be comparatively harmless if drug-using kids simply grew up and out of this "phase"—but many of us don't. And the primary reasons we don't do so are centered in the drugs and the sex in our lives.

Some of us—in my school crowd it must have been close to 25 percent—just kept on using and increasing our intake of alcohol and other drugs, and having sex like crazy all the time. Because we found out how to buy stuff from dealers in town, we moved on from the depressant drugs like pot and alcohol to uppers—amphetamines in pill form, and even to LSD, PCP, cocaine, crack, or to heroin.

I freely admit that I tried them all in my drugging career. I was scared of heroin and only skin-popped it a couple of times—that is injected a very little bit just beneath the skin below my left elbow. I didn't try for a vein. But by the time I was 16 or 17, I used cocaine on a pretty regular basis and loved it.

Cocaine, or any sort of speed, makes you feel really great. I tried many times in the last year to explain the feeling to my parents, but always failed. They listened and told me it sounded a little like drinking coffee. But comparing cocaine to coffee is like comparing Robert Redford to Donald Duck.

When you snort a line of coke at a party, or even just a little snow out of your spoon, you feel on top of everything, full of energy, incredibly optimistic. You think you are going to marry the best guy in the world, have great sex, live in a big house and have a million dollars a year to spend in The Virgin Islands, a Jaguar, respect from everybody— status, status, status.

THE EFFECTS OF DRUGS ON YOUR BODY

Mood-altering drugs affect the central nervous system, by either depressing or stimulating the brain and affecting your behavior. If you keep using those drugs again and again, your body gradually builds up tolerance to them, and demands greater amounts to get the same effect. If you start out getting high on a couple of beers, and like it, after a while you may need a couple of six-packs to get the same high. The same thing applies to any mood-altering drug you use.

When you use several drugs in combination—pot and alcohol, for instance—those drugs "potentiate" or multiply in effect within your system. If you drink on top of downers such as Valium or Quaaludes you may almost double the effects of both the alcohol and the pills, and get much more intoxicated!

Gradually, however, your body becomes accustomed even to this state of being. And before long, your body and your mind do not know how to function without those drugs. You may not be able to eat, sleep, have sex, or concentrate without them. You may not be able to get up in the morning, or go to bed at night without some sort of drug.

When you feel as if you can't get along in life without your drugs, you're hooked, without ever intending to become so. It happens to a large number of young users. And the vast majority of those people—just like me—find themselves hooked not only on alcohol, but on a lot of other stuff: pot, uppers, downers, whatever we've regularly taken into our system.

Then they're in over their heads. At that point, they can do absolutely nothing to recover by themselves. I know from experience. Unless we admit we are addicted and receive help, we'll go crazy or die from the effects of the drugs on our system. I was almost there.

ACTIVITIES FOR YOU

1. Describe your first drink or use of drugs. How did you feel? Did you become high?

2. If your friends—your peers—had not pressured you to drink or use drugs would you have done so on your own?

3. Did you pressure other people to drink or use drugs? Why?

4. How did you react when your parents, teachers, or counselors

tried to stop you from drinking or using, and to change your behavior?

5. What is your favorite drug—your drug of choice?

6. How did you mix drugs and alcohol? Draw a picture to describe how you felt with two or more drugs in your system.

7. If you are in a group, act out for each other the typical way you bought drugs from pushers.

8. If you are in a group, try to act out for each how you behaved when you were really stoned or high on alcohol.

WHAT CAME NEXT IN MY LIFE

Though I managed to finish high school with a D average, both my parents and my teachers knew by that time I was drinking and using. And I didn't care. I was either wired and terribly aggressive, or depressed and totally withdrawn all the time. Though my parents had wanted me to get a college education, I couldn't even think about it. They hoped I would get some sort of job, but I didn't have enough energy to get out of bed in the morning.

My parents and I reached a terrible impasse that is also experienced by countless American families. Parents want their drinking and drugging kids to kick the habit, to get an education, or a job, to get married, and become adults. But users haven't the foggiest notion of what it means to be an adult. How could we?

If we're constantly wasted, how can we possibly accept any responsibilities for work or for other people? When we're using, we don't know from one hour to the next what we're capable of doing.

Under pressure from parents, many users do enroll in college, or get a job, or even get married. And that decision usually lasts about one semester, or a couple of months, or a week and a half. Some of my using friends quickly dropped out of college, jobs, or marriages. I flunked out of a mediocre liberal arts college after one semester. I got all F's.

Strangely enough, many parents and even kids think college, a job, or marriage will cure them of addiction. My closest girl friend from high school got married and convinced her husband he was going to save her from cocaine and whiskey. In the end, they were both wasted.

When I flunked out of college, I felt absolutely desperate, and so did my parents. Because I experienced so much guilt and self-hatred,

I just increased my use of alcohol and coke. For the first time in my life, I began to realize I might never get out of this nightmare. But all I felt like doing then was staying perpetually stoned out of my mind, listening to MTV, and hanging around with other perpetually stoned young people.

The experience is impossible to describe. I was rebellious and hateful toward my parents, but at the same time felt totally helpless and dependent upon them. I despised them for judging me, but was scared to death they might kick me out.

One night at a local bar, a boy named Danny and I decided we had found the way out of our common dilemma. We would get married. I figured if that didn't work, I could become a lesbian. And if that didn't work, I could kill myself.

A MARRIAGE MADE IN HELL

Our marriage was the sorriest time of my life, and the beginning of recovery for me. Danny and I got some money from our parents, eloped, and went on a "honeymoon" in the Blue Ridge Mountains. Supposedly, we were going to drive from Front Royal, Virginia, to Asheville, North Carolina. We got as far as a little Virginia town named, Waynesboro, where we somehow managed to run off the Shenandoah Parkway into the wild blue yonder.

If we hadn't hit a tree, we'd still be sailing down into that valley! We ended up in the hospital with various bumps and bruises, going crazy from drug withdrawal. To this day, I have no idea what those doctors thought they had on their hands.

When we got out of the hospital, we hitchhiked over to Charlottesville, Virginia, on the other side of the mountain, panhandled some money, and managed to buy some coke. We discovered we could get almost as much stuff in that town as we could get in New York City. College towns are like that.

For two months or so we just hung around, pretending to ourselves and our parents that we were having an extended honeymoon. What we were having was an extended freak-out. Day and night we drank, drugged, and had sex.

They say Thomas Jefferson's home, called Monticello, is in Charlottesville. You couldn't prove it by me. Danny and I lived in some room close to the university, but I don't remember a single building or even a campus. I believe the University of Virginia is there because the map says so. Maybe someday I'll visit it.

OFF TO JAIL

During the last week or so, Danny and I were really out of it. I vaguely remember hustling money on the streets, and partying with some strangers. I remember some policemen hassling me somewhere late at night. I woke up in jail.

In Charlottesville, they called it the "Minimum Security Complex." Actually, it wasn't half bad, though at first other inmates snubbed me. When I told them my story, however, they got real respectful. They figured I was streetwise, and were really very good to me.

I got a court-appointed lawyer who told me I had been arrested on an assault and battery charge. At first I thought I had been assaulted, but learned it was the other way around. Apparently, I had beaned some girl over the head with a beer bottle in some dumb little bar. To this day, I can't believe she pressed charges. I acted in self-defense, we later contended.

In any case, we beat the charges, but the judge ordered me to be examined to see if I was a drug addict! I had never been so insulted in my life.

The shrink pronounced me a doper, and admitted me to his treatment program—a state-funded program of the university, I think. I skipped out the first day, caught a ride on Route #29, and kept on going north until I got to my parent's home in New York State.

I never saw Danny, my husband, again. Friends of mine told me he busted out of jail and lit out for LA. Your guess is as good as mine. Though it still hurts to think about, I suspect he's long gone, maybe even dead.

OUT OF THE HOUSE AND INTO TREATMENT

Well, now I was back home and hating it with every fiber of my being, and my parents hated it even more. My father simply refused to talk to me. My mother cried a lot and started sentences with the words, "Well, Holly, we really have to sit down and . . . " But I never let her finish. I had had it.

Somehow, I managed to get money, begging, borrowing, and for the first time in my life, occasionally exchanging sex for drugs. To this day, I can't believe I sank so low. I tried to protect my ego by refusing to sleep with guys who were into kinky stuff. But believe me, discrimination at that low level of existence doesn't count for much. I felt like

I had become a small-town hooker with a habit. I had gone right on down the drain to the bottom.

Since my parents' town has only about 50,000 inhabitants, my father got the delightful news eventually from a policeman friend of his that his wayward daughter was probably selling her body for drugs. Thank God, that was finally enough for him. I really mean that. I was in desperate need of confrontation from my parents. I got it.

One morning early, my father tromped into my bedroom, shook me half awake, and told me he and my mother had committed me for treatment in a center for alcoholics and other addicts out in the country somewhere. I told him to leave me alone and let me sleep. He said, go ahead, but at 11:00 a.m. you're going into the hospital. When he left my room, I reached under my mattress for my pint of whiskey, took a long swallow, and went back to sleep.

At 11:00 a.m., though, I found myself in the admissions office of a treatment center. I was to spend seven weeks in that center—about three more weeks than an average alcoholic spends. I needed every minute of it.

> *I was rebellious and hateful toward my parents, but at the same time felt totally helpless and dependent upon them.*

What I learned and experienced in that center completely changed my life. In fact, I owe my life both to the staff and my fellow patients in that center—and to all the people I have since met in Alcoholics Anonymous and Narcotics Anonymous. I owe my life and well-being to my dad, and to a Higher Power who somehow watched over me even when I had screwed up everything, my education, my marriage, my early chances for a "career," my morals, and my health.

RECOVERY!

You or your parents may be afraid of treatment at first, but don't worry. For the first couple of days or weeks, the whole program seems impossible.

All of us who experience recovery from addiction come to the realization we have lost power over the drugs, but can't manage our lives without them. When I became slowly convinced of that fact, I also became convinced I needed help from every possible person, resource, and power source outside myself to learn how to exist without booze and other addictive chemicals.

For three or four weeks, I didn't seem to sleep, my muscles cramped endlessly, I had diarrhea day and night, hemorrhoids, a faulty bladder, headaches, and the "screaming meemies."

Fortunately for me, the nurses and everyone else on the staff knew I was going through the dreadful business of withdrawing from alcohol, cocaine, and a wide variety of tranquilizers simultaneously. Let me tell you right now: withdrawal from downers is worse than kicking heroin. The pits! You make it only because compassionate staff members and fellow patients—some of whom have gone through the same stuff—keep telling you you'll get better.

After about a month, however, I began to feel almost blissfully relieved of drug influence. I came to believe that by faith in other recovering people and in a Higher Power, whom today I call the God of my understanding, I could learn how to live without drugs. I could learn how to replace the drugs in my life with loving people, good goals, and the joy of responsible and moral behavior.

I hadn't given God a serious thought since I was thirteen. Groups of people honestly discussing serious things like responsible behavior and character improvement would a year earlier have driven me up a wall. Now, I came to realize in a matter of a few short weeks that I needed all those people and all those things as badly as I needed the air I breathed.

I latched on with my last gasp. And by God's help and the help of so many people in AA and NA, I haven't had a drink, a mood-altering pill, a snort of coke, a bag, or a joint, for almost two years.

NEW LIFE

I went back to college to finish a two-year program in business. I got a job in my hometown in a local hospital. I plan next to go to school part-time to complete a B.S. in business. I have high hopes, ultimately, of getting either an M.B.A. or a C.P.A. I have a boyfriend, and I think eventually we'll get married. He's a recovering cross-addicted person just like me, and, believe it or not, is an R.N. in the hospital where I work.

My relationship with my parents has never been better. I can't tell you how grateful I am for my new feelings toward them. Together we know the drugs had us licked, but we didn't know what to do about it. My father finally just reached out blindly, stuck me into a treatment center, and so initiated the road to recovery for the whole family.

I'd be lying if I said everything has gone perfectly since my treatment experience. Recovery from addiction doesn't solve life's problems for you, but gives you a sober and straight mind to deal with them. I have some health problems related to my years of drug consumption. My boyfriend and I are basically broke. Some of the people in town still remember I hustled on the streets, and avoid me. And that's tough for me to handle. But as they continue to see me straight and well, I notice even they begin to forget.

And in the AA or NA groups I attend every night of the week, I have some of the closest and best friends, male and female, any person could ever hope for. I'm able to pray every day and night, and many times during the day, and just say, Thanks God, for life, for peace of mind, for loving parents, for a supportive and understanding boyfriend, for all my friends, for the food I eat, for the sleep I now get without drugs, for the air I breathe.

WHAT CAN YOU DO?

All in all, I feel very lucky and very grateful. And believe me, if you're currently using and boozing, you can feel the same if only you reach out to others for help. If you're slipping down the drain, look in your phone book, call AA, and ask for someone to talk to. It won't cost you a thing. All you have to do is listen.

Or get a schedule of AA or NA meetings in your area, and attend. one. You don't have to say or do a thing at meetings. All you have to do is listen.

If you feel really low, talk to someone at your nearest treatment center for alcoholism and drug addiction. In this country, there are so many good treatment centers and I know there's one near you. Someone will listen to you, and tell you what help you need, and whether you can and should go into treatment.

And if you're a parent reading this book, I urge you to move on to my parents' contributions to this series, the next chapter, "Young and Restless—For Parents Only." I know I'm prejudiced, but I think it's the best chapter in the book. My parents helped to write it.

And as Red Skelton used to say in closing, "God Bless!"

Questions for: *Young and Restless—For the Young Person*

1. Did you experiment with alcohol, nicotine, and other drugs at an early age? Describe your experiences.

2. The author of this booklet says she intitally drank and used drugs to impress other people, and to get along easily with members of the opposite sex. Have you had similar experiences? Explain.

3. The author thinks that drug abuse by young people often causes poor relationships with their parents. If this has happened to you, describe your experiences.

4. Some addicted young people have alcoholic and/or abusive parents. If you think you have such parents, how can you come to terms with them, and still avoid alcohol and other drugs?

5. If you used alcohol and similar drugs to socialize or have sex, how do you propose to develop a social life without drugs?

6. If most of your close friends are alcoholics or drug users, do you think you can go back to their company? Explain. If you want to find new friends, where can you turn?

7. The girl telling the story had some pretty bad experiences in jail, in a mental institution, on the streets, and in her sex life. Have you had similarly bad experiences? If not, how can her story still be helpful for you in recovery?

15

Young and Restless—For Parents Only

INTRODUCTION

Whenever parents of adolescents, teenagers, or young adults gather socially today, someone is almost bound to bring up the "drug problem" among younger people—a problem all responsible parents fear may emerge within their own family circle. Not only do parents read and hear about the problem in society at large; they gradually learn about it from their own children and their friends. If the parents drink or use other drugs themselves, they may even, without intending to do so, introduce their children to the abuse of alcohol and similar mood-altering drugs.

It has become proverbial by now to say that the problem of alcoholism and addiction among teenagers and young adults crosses class, gender, and racial lines. It has become equally proverbial to say that older adults, by and large, do not know as much as they need to know about addictive disorders. Both statements are true. This chapter has been written by a mother, who along with her husband, learned about drug abuse among teenagers the hard way. The teenager they describe is their own daughter. They have written the chapter in order to help others avoid the mistakes they made in trying to cope with this problem: addiction among the young.

OUR STORY

We are the parents of an addicted child named Holly. Holly has written one of the chapters in *The High Road* from her perspective as a recovering drug addict. We shall now attempt to write from our perspective as parents of a terribly sick young woman who by God's grace and the help of the wonderful programs of Alcoholics Anonymous and Narcotics Anonymous is today free from drugs and alcohol.

We have found it very difficult to write of our experiences. Many of them are deeply personal and bring pain to us as we recall them and try to put them into words.

However, since we have become involved in Families Anonymous and Al-Anon, companion organizations to AA for family members of addicted persons, we have come to realize that many American parents are today experiencing the very pain we experienced. We hope and pray that our story will be helpful for you, and give you reason for hope of recovery with your own family.

THE EARLY YEARS

We are what journalists, I suppose, would call "middle-Americans." Since we both have paying jobs, we have a comfortable family income. We are buying a home, have a number of older but adequate cars, and enough money to enjoy not only the necessities but some of the luxuries of life. We are active members of a small and very friendly Episcopal parish, and consider ourselves to be rather traditional Christian people.

We live in a medium-sized town in upstate New York. Though many families in our town have in recent years fallen apart, and though, as we were to discover, both the drug and prostitution trades flourish underground in our town, we nonetheless lead, by and large, rather quiet lives. We had no reason whatsoever to anticipate in advance the problems our daughter experienced.

. . . beware of explaining sudden changes in children's behavior by pretending . . . they are going through a "phase" . . . of life.

When she went to high school we fully expected her to do well in preparation for college, a good job, and marriage to come. Since we both graduated with college degrees, we simply took it for granted that Holly would want to do the same.

At first she did. In her ninth-grade year, she got good grades, became active in the drama club, seemed highly motivated, and had a wonderful set of girl friends, many of them children of parents in our own social group.

Sometime in the tenth grade, however, Holly seemed almost overnight to lose interest in her studies, and in extracurricular activities she had previously enjoyed. She also decided she didn't like her former set of girl friends anymore. Though we were disappointed in her behavior and vaguely worried about her change of mood, we nonetheless decided she was going through a phase.

She was, after all, barely through puberty, and had developed an interest in boys only very recently. As we talked with close friends about our problems, we more or less decided that she would pass through this stage with flying colors.

EARLY WARNING SIGNALS

1. First Warning—The Big Change. Beware of sudden changes in children's behavior. Beware of pretending to yourself that they are going through a "phase" or "stage" of life. Through Al-Anon, we have discovered that the so-called adolescent phase of life in our country is often complicated by alcohol and other drug consumption. Your changing child just may be changing in part because he or she is consuming mood-altering chemicals. Because our daughter was doing just that, she entered a "phase" which could very well have ended in her early death.

Within a few months, Holly literally stopped studying for her classes, gave up her interest in school plays, began missing many classes due to vague illnesses, and began staying out late at night with friends she didn't want to introduce to us.

We tried to rationalize all of this peculiar behavior, but had great difficulty with the late hours and unidentified friends. Holly was, after all, only about 15 at the time. Although the phase theory might explain her sudden loss of interest in school, we did not think it explained her need to stay out late and run around with friends she refused to identify to us.

*Both of us lacked the simple courage
to take parental responsibility for her
life . . .*

2. Second Warning—Outright Intoxication. One Friday night we waited up for Holly to come home. She rolled in about 2:00 a.m., and we mean literally rolled. Since she could barely walk, she virtually fell through the front door into my husband's arms. And, in fact, had he not caught her she would, I think, have simply collapsed on the floor.

At first we assumed she was sick, and we asked her anxiously what the matter was. Instead of telling us, however, she suddenly burst into anger, hit my husband with her fist right on his cheek, and screamed: "Don't you ever ask me what's wrong. It's none of your damn business!" And then she wobbled off to her room and slammed the door.

Needless to say, we were completely stunned. So we ran to her door and knocked. Holly told us, sharply, to "Go f--- yourselves." I am not making this up. Never in our lives had we heard her speak that word before. Now she screamed it at us.

At that point, my husband and I both became angry, and bolted through the door into her room. We found Holly flat out on her back on her bed. Her face seemed gray, and yet was splotched with angry red patches. Her small room reeked with alcohol.

Simultaneously, we said, "Holly, you're drunk." She opened her eyes then, stared at me, but seemed to have difficulty focusing on me. Weakly, she said, "Yeah, mom, I'm drunk. I won't do it again." And she passed out.

Well, you parents who have had similar experiences can guess what we did. Together we decided to ground Holly for a month (it turned out to be only a week), and would give her a lecture on the dangers of drunkenness, especially if she was socializing with people who drove cars. We also laid down the law about hours. From that time on Holly was supposed to stay home on weeknights to study, and on weekends had to be home by midnight. We furthermore insisted that we had to meet her friends.

But curiously relieved, we also decided that she was still going through her "phase," now complicated by a little teenage "experimentation" with alcohol. After all, we reasoned, didn't all young people try to drink beer? Hadn't we experimented with beer?

Though we had to admit we hadn't really drunk much until we were in college, and had rarely become drunk, we were nonetheless almost happy to believe that Holly was passing through an almost necessary, perhaps even healthy, stage of growing up by trying alcohol. That was a very dangerous and almost fatal mistake.

3. Third Warning—Rapid Deterioration. A year passed and Holly did not grow up, but down. In spite of repeated talks with her, with her teachers and school counselors, Holly's grades continued to nose-dive. In the 11th grade, she considered herself lucky to get D's—which I think some of the teachers gave to her simply out of consideration for us, their friends.

Incredibly, Holly didn't seem to give a hoot what grades she got. All she talked about was getting out of school, or even dropping out, "being true to herself," and having "fun." What she wanted to do with her life was totally unclear, it seemed, both to her and to us.

Whenever we tried to get her interested in school activities, she seemed to become outraged at us. Though we tried to be strict about her hours, she frequently sneaked out on weeknights, and regularly came in past midnight on weekends. Again and again, we grounded her, only to see her do the same things all over again within a few weeks. Whenever we tried to discover more about the "friends," she became angry at us. In fact, when we attempted to discuss her overall decline, she became outraged, almost on schedule.

4. Fourth Warning—Temper Tantrums. Beware of your children's outbursts of temper and outrage. Since we know that Holly was by now completely addicted to alcohol and other drugs, and running around with other similarly addicted people, we know also that she often feigned outrage at our questions simply to shut us up, or throw us off the track. And we were, in fact, grossly intimidated by our own daughter. Both of us lacked the simple courage to take parental responsibility for her life, to find out in a forthright manner what was going on, and to take steps to help her.

We have discovered in Families Anonymous and Al-Anon that large numbers of parents do fear their own children. We fear their temper tamtrums; we're scared that stern discipline from us might somehow "damage" their personalities permanently. We're afraid we might lose their love.

Whereas, our parents disciplined us very strictly—at times, too strictly—but usually with love, we parents decided, under social pressure, that discipline somehow ran counter to love. We were wrong. And as a result, both we and our daughter had many years of incredible suffering yet to come.

LAST STRAW—NUMBER ONE

One night my husband worked late at his office and chose to take a walk on one of our main streets to clear his head. As he walked he saw a gang of teenagers, some with motorcycles, gathered near an alleyway off the street. Many of the youngsters were talking loudly; one of them had a noisy radio, loudly blaring away.

Thinking to quiet the group down, and to get them to go home, my husband walked toward the youngsters. Immediately, they stopped talking. One of the boys in the group advanced on my husband, and said "What do you want, pops?" or something like that, and waved a bicycle chain ominously in the air above his head. Though startled, my husband kept cool and simply said, "I think you're out kind of late."

At that, the entire group burst out laughing, hooting and hollering at him, and slapping each other on the backs. In fact, one of the boys slapped another so hard that he literally fell on his face. And at that point, my husband realized that all the group members were either drunk or drugged on something. So he said, "You kids are drunk. Now go on home or I'm calling the police."

At that a female voice said very loudly, "Oh daddy, don't be such a s--t!" And everyone laughed loudly again and moved on down the alleyway.

Stunned, my husband recognized the voice of our own daughter. Even in the dim alley light, he could see her pale but leering face. Because he was shocked, however, he stood rooted to the ground as the group disappeared.

> . . . if your children are addicted, they cannot, without help, change their behavior.

THE PERMANENT CHANGE

After my husband arrived home, we decided to wait up and confront Holly with the evidence we had inadvertently accumulated. For the first time, we became fully aware of something we had suspected but repressed for some time: Holly was drinking and probably using drugs.

Holly was running around with a gang of kids who often acted like a punk rock group, complete with motorcycles, leather clothes, and chains.

When our daughter did try to sneak through the back door at about 4:00 a.m., we were there to confront her. Though angry, she didn't seem the least bit surprised. Obviously, she and her friends had anticipated our presence. In fact, both my husband and I would swear afterwards that some of those friends actually stood in the back-yard behind Holly, fairly close to the door.

We closed the door, and my husband said "Holly, tomorrow we're going to take you to the hospital for a checkup, and maybe for treatment. We believe you've been drinking and using drugs for years, and probably need help to get off of them."

Well, I can hardly describe what happened next. First, Holly flew into a rage and knocked one of our den lamps down and stamped on it, smashing it into pieces. Next she rolled on the floor like a little child, throwing a temper tantrum. Finally, she crawled forward and began chewing my husband's ankle! It was as if our daughter had suddenly gone stark raving mad.

My husband reached down, pulled Holly to her feet. Suddenly, Holly collapsed into his arms and began weeping uncontrollably, begging for forgiveness, and promising in blubbering terms we could scarcely understand that she would give up the drugs, and alcohol and all her friends.

"I've had enough, Daddy," she said, and cradled herself in his arms. "I'm going to change my whole life. You'll see."

And like fools, we realize now, we quickly changed our mood. Our anger gave way to pity and the real love we felt toward Holly. Since we wanted so badly to believe that she could give up this kind of life, we forced ourselves to believe so.

5. Fifth Warning—Promises Are Not Enough. When your addicted child promises—probably in good faith—to reform himself or herself, to stop drinking and drugging on his own, and to find new friends, try not to believe what you hear. That sounds brutal, but if your children are addicted, they cannot, without help, change their behavior. In withdrawal from drugs, they will feel not only as if they are going crazy, but also that they have no way of coping with life without drugs.

Furthermore, when they give up their drugs, they must also give up an entire set of friends they now depend upon. Most young people cannot even begin by themselves to make such changes, let alone complete them.

THE VICIOUS CIRCLE

Because of the pain we might cause ourselves and Holly, we find it best just to skim over the surface of the following years in her life. Somehow, Holly managed barely to finish high school, and after doing a stint in summer school, was belatedly given a diploma. Though the school officials did not allow her to participate in her own graduation, she didn't seem to mind a bit, but went out to "celebrate" with a number of her classmates who failed to graduate.

She came home the next morning totally drunk and disoriented. When we asked what had happened, she said she had been in a "beauty contest" and went off to her room, where she collapsed in bed and slept for about the next 24 hours.

> *. . . you will not be able to help them toward recovery by love alone. Those children need very direct confrontation.*

Years later Holly told us she had been partying, and probably "had sex" with some of the boys. Only years later were we to discover that heavy drug consumption and "free sex" usually went hand in hand in her group. And though at first my husband became very angry at the boys for taking advantage of the girls, we realize now that everybody "took advantage" of everyone else. In fact, in that twilight world of addiction, nobody realized fully what they were doing, but reached out blindly for pleasure through sex just as they did with the drugs.

That event initiated a string of similar events altogether too night-marish even to describe. Not only could we no longer predict when Holly would come home at night, we could not predict what shape she would be in. Always she was half-drunk, or, as we later came to learn, half drugged on a variety of drugs: cocaine, amphetamines, LSD, barbiturates and tranquilizers.

If you live in a small town or in the country, don't imagine your children can't get the drugs they want to try or use. Any young person in any part of the country can get drugs if they are wanted badly enough. And lots of people, young and older, sell them illegally, at a good profit. In fact, most users of illegal drugs eventually sell them to get enough money to keep using them.

Somewhere along the line, Holly eloped with one of her drunken and drugged friends, and disappeared with him for months in a Virginia town we never visited. In that town, she apparently drank and used drugs almost non-stop, associated with the wildest sorts of people, got into a fight one night in a bar with another young woman, and ended up for a while in jail!

After a lawyer got her out of jail, she was committed for observation in a psychiatric ward, from which she promptly escaped and came back home to us.

Since we were so happy to see her again, we decided to take her back and try to rehabilitate her with tender loving care, but to no avail. Because we loved her, we decided also to shield her from any further problems in Virginia.

6. Sixth Warning—Love May Not Be Enough. No matter how much tender loving care you have to offer to your addicted children, you will not be able to help them toward recovery by love alone. It sounds awful, but it is true. Those children need very direct confrontation, usually from family members as well as people outside the family, in order to realize how desperately sick they are.

LAST STRAW—NUMBER TWO

The real last straw came for us when a businessman and good friend told us one evening over the phone that he had reason to believe that our daughter might both be selling drugs and getting them from other pushers—"salesmen," he called them—in our town for the price of sex.

Though shocked, we both knew now what we had to do. Since our daughter was not only addicted to drugs, but perhaps liable to prosecution for selling them, we simply had to commit her for treatment. Because of contacts we had already made, we decided that very night we would call the center the next morning, make a reservation, and place her. If she protested, we were ready to obtain a court order to have her committed.

Try your . . . best to maintain good communication with your children during their difficult adolescent years.

When my husband confronted our daughter the next morning, she was too drunk or drugged or something, even to protest. At about noon that day, we drove her to the treatment center. With a tremendous sense of relief and accomplishment, we left her there, and went home.

RECOVERY FOR ALL

As the days went by, we discovered that we also were expected to become patients at the center. Since our daughter was sick with addiction, we also had become sick with her—trying to protect ourselves while all the time enabling her to continue her drinking and drugging.

As she began to accept treatment, so also did we. Since we were told we must for our own sake attend open meetings of Alcoholics Anonymous and closed meetings of Al-Anon or Families Anonymous we did so, and discovered to our great surprise and joy that some of our closest friends in our town belonged either to AA or Al-Anon, and sometimes to both. We also attended some open meetings of Narcotics Anonymous in New York City, and anticipated the time when Holly would attend the one NA group available in our own town.

With treatment, and with attendance at what is now our own beloved home group of Al-Anon, we began ever so slightly to hope and to believe that Holly and we could recover from this terrible nightmare.

Over a year and a half have passed since Holly entered treatment. By God's grace and the help of the AA program, Holly has been, we believe, free from alcohol and all other mood-altering drugs since that time. She has a good job in one of our local hospitals, and is attending a community college, hoping eventually to complete a four-year degree at a New York State university.

Like all alcoholics and similar addicts, however, Holly remains susceptible to drug abuse for the rest of her life. Though abstinence from drugs arrests the progress of addiction, neither abstinence nor the AA program ever makes it possible for a dependent person to use alcohol or other mood-altering drugs socially again.

Because, however, we believe both in the power of God, and the marvelous people in AA and Al-Anon, we have high hopes that both our daughter and we shall be able from this time forth to lead relatively normal and healthy lives.

TIPS FOR PARENTS

In summary, to avoid many of the grievous mistakes we made over the years with Holly, we urge you to consider the following:

1. Try your best to maintain good communication with your children during their difficult adolescent years.

2. As you talk to them about adulthood, however, try also to convey your own feelings and convictions about human behavior, morality, and spirituality.

3. Even if you sense that your children resist your ethics—especially in the areas of sex or alcohol and drug use—stand lovingly firm in your conversations with them.

No matter how they may react at the moment, we know now that Holly needed moral guidelines from us, and limits for her behavior, which we failed to set. Our children need a firm and powerful model for adulthood which they can both challenge and copy.

If you are active in a church fellowship, for instance, we believe you should encourage your children to remain active also, even after adolescence. For in healthy church settings, children may discover not only responsible adults they admire, but peers who follow a reasonably disciplined and spiritual way of life.

4. If your child undergoes what seems to be a pronounced personality change right after adolescence, try to find out whether he or she is drinking or drugging on a regular basis. Though personality changes obviously occur in the life of every teenager, drugs greatly magnify those changes.

5. If your child suddenly switches from one set of friends to another, and seems to shield the latter from your view, you have every reason to be deeply suspicious of drug and alcohol abuse—and sexual license as well. Your children feel guilty about such behavior, and will automatically try to protect themselves and their drugging friends from your judgments.

In their own group they build up peer power to rationalize their own behavior, and to resist any adverse pressures they might receive from parents, school, or society.

---

*If you know your child is getting
drunk or drugged on a regular
basis . . . seek help immediately.*

---

6. If your child seems suddenly to lose interest in schoolwork and extracurricular activities, you have good reason to suspect the possibility of drug abuse. Though many children show their growing pains by rebelling against teachers and classes, many of those rebellious children also use drugs. The drugs reduce a child's motivation for school (really life's work), and also mask feelings of guilt and insecurity which develop as he or she begins to fail.

7. If you know your child is getting drunk or drugged on a regular basis, or keeps alcohol, drugs, or drug paraphernalia in his or her room, seek help immediately through a visit to a counselor in your local treatment center, or through attendance at Al-Anon or Families Anonymous meetings. A good drug counselor or a long-time Al-Anon parent of addicted young persons will tell you about the various types of paraphernalia to watch out for.

Hope is just a phone call away.

If you become convinced your child is abusing drugs, try with the help of your family members, perhaps a treatment center staff person, your minister or doctor, and maybe a school counselor, to arrange a meeting to confront your child with the evidences of addiction and so induce him or her to seek treatment.

Above all, if your children have trouble, seek help for yourselves in Al-Anon or Families Anonymous. There you will learn how to distance and "detach" yourselves to a degree from your children's problems, so that you may stabilize your own emotions and also stop enabling them to buy and use drugs. We know many parents in Al-Anon whose children continue to drink and drug. Those parents, however, find the strength in their Al-Anon groups, and from a God they come to depend upon, to lead relatively healthy lives in spite of their children's illnesses.

And please, do not lose hope in the face of your children's problems. Fifty years ago, you and they would probably have been doomed to slow and painful deterioration. With the coming of AA, Al-Anon, treatment programs, and more recently, NA and Families Anonymous, there is help and hope.

Hope is just a phone call away. Hope is just a meeting away. If you're hurting right now, feeling hopeless and helpless, contact AA or Al-Anon. Go to an Al-Anon meeting tonight. Attend an open AA meeting and learn about the illness your child experiences. Get in touch with an alcoholism treatment facility to see if it has a family program. It just may be the first day of an entirely new life for you and all the members of your family.

Questions for: *Young And Restless—For Parents Only*

1. The parents of this young addicted person made several basic mistakes as they tried to cope with her early addictive behavior. What were those mistakes? Have you also made similar mistakes? Explain.

2. In this story, the addicted girl early in high school experienced marked behavioral changes. Describe the behavioral changes you or your children experienced after they began drinking and using drugs.

3. Why does a parent's "tender, loving care" in itself usually fail to help an addicted young family member toward recovery?

4. Why do you think so many parents today are afraid to confront their chldren over poor behavior, and to take steps to bring about changes in their lives? Describe your own experiences.

5. What events or circumstances finally induced you to confront your children and seek help for them?

6. Have you ever attended Al-Anon or open AA meetings? What benefits could you obtain by attending such meetings on a regular basis?

16

In The End Is A Beginning
Index

INTRODUCTION

The writers of this chapter try to help alcoholics or addicts realize that they cannot find a "cure" for their addiction without help from resources outside themselves. Members of Alcoholics Anonymous and staff members at treatment centers for addictive disorders often call this realization "working the First Step."

Addiction is a terminal illness which renders the drug user powerless over the chemicals he or she consumes. Like other terminal diseases, the person affected must accept the reality of the illness before anyone else can provide him help. Addiction, however, is unique among all illnesses in that the addicted person must come to believe that he is "powerless" over the very chemicals upon which he has come to depend. As long as an addicted person believes he is in control of the alcohol and drugs he uses, he will reject others who try to help him gain relief from addiction.

The addicted person develops this attitude in part because he clings to the illusion that he can control his consumption. If he is addicted, however, that is precisely what he cannot do. In this chapter, you will discover why. You will also discover how the end of the road for an alcoholic—loss of control over alcohol—is usually the beginning of a new way of life.

FIVE QUESTIONS

Before you start the chapter, answer the following questions honestly. If you answer one "yes," you have special reasons for reading further.

1. Do you regularly feel that you should cut down on your alcohol or drug consumption?

2. Have your family members, close friends, or employer said that you should cut down on your drinking or drugging?

3. Do you often consume more alcohol or other drugs than you intend to?

4. Have you driven drunk more than once, or performed other acts under the influence of alcohol or other drugs?

5. Have you *more than once* forgotten what you did and said (blacked out) while you were conscious but intoxicated on alcohol or other drugs?

POWER LOSS

It begins with a power loss. We alcoholics lose power over our drinking. We drink more than we really intend to drink. We drink at the wrong times and do irresponsible things which no one—an alcoholic least of all—desires or admires.

Alcoholics drink for a purpose, in a pattern, and with preoccupation. Typically, we drink to cope with realities of life, to escape from pain, anxiety, and other uncomfortable feelings, and then we feel guilty about it. The more guilty we feel, the more we drink, and in the long run the more tense and depressed we get.

When an alcoholic drinks, he or she knows that alcohol hurts him or her and others. The thought usually depresses us. The thought also drives us to another drink, which makes us all the more depressed, which drives us to yet another drink. And so on. We alcoholics do not decide to become alcoholic or addicted to other drugs. We literally lose control and we cannot by our own power regain control.

Some of us are born with a genetic predisposition toward alcoholism. Some of us grow up in families which dispose us toward heavy drinking. Some of us drink so much over such a long period of time that we simply lose control over our consumption and become addicted.

We alcoholics seem, also, to gain from alcohol a profound sense of relief and elation which non-alcoholics do not experience. Whatever the causes, all alcoholics lose control over their alcohol consumption, and consequently over their own patterns of behavior.

The vast majority discover that we cannot by ourselves stop drinking or drugging for good. Ultimately we drink out of an uncontrollable need for the effects of alcohol, thus undermining our capacities both for responsible work and for loving relationships with people, or even with the God of our understanding.

Alcoholism is a diabolical illness, a state of living death. We alcoholics try to resolve through alcohol the agonies we create through alcohol. In some sense we know it, and yet we keep on drinking.

> *We . . . do not decide to become alcoholic . . . we literally lose control . . . we cannot by our own power regain control.*

Our sober family members and friends hope we will stop drinking in a destructive manner. And though deep down inside we also want to stop drinking in that manner, we simply cannot do what everyone wants us to do. Because our body, mind, and emotions all tell us we need alcohol, we lose the power to give it up on our own. We feel driven to drink.

That's a real mess! What can we do about it? By ourselves, we alcoholics can do one thing.

THE ONE THING NEEDED

We can admit we are "powerless over alcohol," that our lives have become "unmanageable." If we can't admit that obvious truth, we can't do anything else about our problems. If we don't believe we're powerless over alcohol, we'll continue to use alcohol until we go crazy or die, usually of alcohol-related illnesses.

Nothing, however, comes harder for us than admission of the obvious, and for good reason. No human being likes to admit defeat. No alcoholic wants to admit he's beaten by alcohol. If I lack self-control over alcohol, how can I continue to live? If I admit loss of control over alcohol, what happens next?

All adults, alcoholics included, pride themselves on self-control, initiative, and the ability to achieve success through willpower and hard work. Americans in particular admire self-made and self-reliant men or women dependent upon no one but themselves. More than any other people in the world, we want to believe that everyone can achieve the grand goal of American life: personal success by individual effort.

Isn't that true for you?

We alcoholics, however, have discovered very painfully that we cannot achieve our goals through mere personal effort. By ourselves we shall not become a success. We shall become drunk! By ourselves we fail; yet we dread further failure more than anything else in the world. If we can't overcome failure by ourselves, where can we turn?

WHAT COMES NEXT?

Through experience, we alcoholics discover we have to turn to power resources greater than ourselves for help. By necessity, most of us turn to people in a position to help us, and to a Higher Power, whom many of us come to call God. Since the word, "God," makes some people today feel awkward, angry, or embarrassed, we shall in this chapter concentrate on the process of what AA and NA call "turning our will and lives" over to God whom we come to understand and accept.

Please note: If you are an alcoholic or addict, we believe you will also need a Power greater than yourself for recovery—a God whom you can understand. We make this claim, not as clergy persons, or even as "religious people" (many of us claim no religion at all), but as addicted people who have discovered the need for a Higher Power for recovery.

As people powerless over alcohol and drugs, we came to believe that only a Power greater than ourselves could restore us to sobriety and a new way of living. Based on personal experience, we believe that a Higher Power will also become necessary for your recovery. If you can't find a Power greater than yourself to help you manage your life, you risk turning for help to that deceptive god, alcohol, or to other drugs, for relief.

WHERE IS A GOD WHOM WE CAN UNDERSTAND?

How and where do alcoholics find a God who will supply continuing power for living?

In the early phases of recovery most of us alcoholics depend by necessity and quite naturally upon people as sources of power. We depend upon counselors, doctors, pastors, AA groups, and sponsors for help. With a desperation born from defeat by alcohol, we gladly lean on others.

Because people are not available to us every moment of our recovery, we alcoholics also discover, especially in private times of personal power failure, that we require for a happy sobriety a sustaining and ever-present God.

In the early phases of recovery, however, many alcoholics discover they simply have *no faith in God.* In fact, alcoholics from strict religious backgrounds often reject a god who seemed only to threaten and condemn them in the past.

If you're one of those alcoholics, don't worry unduly about your present lack of faith. Instead, follow the advice of alcoholics who have found paths of spiritual recovery for themselves.

Alcoholics who are truly serious about recovery and spiritual growth offer us the following suggestions in our search for the secrets of sobriety.

1. Do not try to force upon yourself a god who makes you feel merely uncomfortable—a threatening god whom you may have rejected while you were growing up, or a god you're too embarrassed to talk about. You cannot go back to a god of the past who seems childish or rejecting of you.

2. Do not try to create a god out of thin air to make you "feel good" for a few moments. As you read magazine articles or books about "spirituality," be careful that others do not force spiritual values upon you which seem unreal or destructive.

3. Listen carefully to the opinions and convictions about spiritual reality expressed by people close to you in your family, social group, church, or recovering fellowship.

We have found it fairly easy to tell the difference between mere "preaching" or moralizing, and the expression of true spiritual experience. Those in your family, social group, church, or recovering groups, who have real spiritual experiences, have something to share with you. As you continue in your sobriety, you will recognize who these people are.

4. When you come to believe in a God who seems real and accepts

you for what you are, you may begin, as in the AA motto, to "let go, let God." You will stop trying to manage life on your own, and let the God of your understanding be the manager of your life day by day. Your faith in a God who directs you will rapidly translate into a humble faith in yourself.

5. Pray for help from a Higher Power, even if you don't for the moment believe or feel there is such a power.

In their struggles for a relationship with God some alcoholics like to say: "Fake it till you make it." We agree with their advice. When you try to follow the example of others who have found spiritual help, you already prove that you at least trust them. You also demonstrate by your behavior that you want to recover by whatever means are available to you.

6. When you pray, ask above all for sobriety. When you are sober, God can fulfill your deepest needs and make you reasonably happy. If you are drunk God can't even reach you, let alone relieve your needs. The bottle is the best hiding place in the world from God!

THE POWER OF PRAYER

In order that you may remain soberly grateful day by day, pray for serenity and peace of mind. Though you may not experience anything close to serenity at a given time or on a given day, God will give you some relief and strength, and above all, give you the power to remain sober.

Pray for a style of life which brings peace without unnecessary strain. No words are more important for the recovering alcoholic than the simple motto, "Easy Does It." In scriptural language, ask for the "peace which surpasses all understanding."

Pray for success in your life, but only for that variety which contributes to your sobriety. Good and loving family relationships always contribute to sobriety. As the Eleventh Step of AA says: Sought through prayer and meditation to improve our conscious contact with God *as we understood Him,* praying only for knowledge of His will for us and the power to carry that out.*

*From Chapter 5 of *Alcoholics Anonymous.* Reprinted with Permission.

SHARING YOUR NEEDS

Try to share your needs with others, especially in meetings of Alcoholics Anonymous.

Through experience, we alcoholics
discover we have to turn to a power
greater than ourselves for help.

Early in recovery you may find yourself shy, nervous, and withdrawn. Because of very real failures in life, you may feel no one will find you acceptable. In AA, however, you will find people who have experienced the same failures but have recovered their spiritual balance. To learn from them, you must try to share your failures with them.

Most alcoholics believe God works through other people to give spiritual success to failed people. Failures shared are failures shed, while hidden failures fester.

When you talk with other people, worry as little as possible about nervousness or lack of speaking ability. Other people can accept your nervousness. When you worry too much about your nerves and the impression you make on others, you merely prove yourself to be destructively self-centered.

Your worries over the impression you make on others always undermine your ability to share yourself with others. Share yourself boldly, and you will be surprised to learn that others want to share themselves also.

In AA . . . you will find people
who . . . have recovered their spiritual
balance. To learn from them, you
must try to share your failures . . .

LEARNING TO LISTEN

Try to listen to people who already have a relationship with a Higher Power. Learn from them what you can do to develop a similar relationship.

Remember, we look for a source of personal power to overcome the powerlessness of our drinking or drugging. When another person possesses a power we lack, we discover through him or her that a power greater than ourselves is available to us also. Through our own listening we find that most spiritually mature people have a daily discipline of spiritual exercise that we may easily follow.

Thousands of recovering alcoholics have a million times over prayed the Serenity Prayer: "God grant me the serenity to accept the things I cannot change, courage to change the things I can, and the wisdom to know the difference." Consider this prayer as part of your day.

NOW IS THE TIME FOR ACTION

If you find yourself out of laziness or disbelief resisting a spiritual discipline, remember how much effort and expense you put into your drinking, into lies about your drinking, and into your medical or legal costs. Remember all the chances you took when drunk.

If you put a fraction of the effort and risk you once expended upon an alcoholic way of death into a spiritual way of life, you could very well become a spiritual giant.

Sobriety neither solves all the problems of life, nor provides anyone automatic meaning in life. As the AA founders, however, said in so many different ways: sobriety is a means to an end—a happy life lived serenely in relationship to a God *whom we understand,* and with people who love and respect us.

God grant me the serenity to accept
the things I cannot change, courage to
change the things I can, and the wis-
dom to know the difference.

A WORD OF HOPE

We offer one word of encouragement to alcoholics only: as an alcoholic powerless over alcohol, with an unmanageable life, you have one great spiritual advantage over seemingly self-reliant people. You know you need a power greater than yourself for continuing recovery. Though you may not think so now, you will have reason ultimately to be thankful for that need.

Recovering alcoholics secure in God are some of the happiest people in the world. To use Dr. Karl Menninger's famous phrase, they are "weller than well," healthier in recovery from illness than they could ever have been without the illness.

God helps not so much those who help themselves, but rather those who need him and ask for help. God gives power to powerless people like us. If you think you're one of us, you have all the reason in the world to hope for recovery.

Who knows? You may also become "weller than well"!

Questions for: *In The End Is A Beginning*

1. If you admit you are powerless over alcohol or other drugs, where do you think you can find power for recovery?

2. When you discover from the Twelve Steps of AA that recovering alcoholics benefit from a God they understand, what comes to your mind when you hear the word, "God"? If God seems unreal or nonexistent to you, what can you do?

3. For many recovering alcoholics and other addicts, an AA or other self-help group becomes a "Higher Power," able to help them "turn over" problems they cannot handle by themselves during recovery. If you do not believe in God, can an AA or other self-help group become a "Higher Power" for you during recovery?

4. Read the Serenity Prayer in this booklet. Explain the prayer in your own words.

5. In AA there is a saying, "Let Go, Let God," by which members mean, let go of your life and its problems, and let God become your manager. Discuss what meaning the saying could have in your life during recovery.